ALSO BY ELISSA ALTMAN

Motherland: A Memoir of Love, Loathing, and Longing

*Poor Man's Feast: A Love Story of Comfort, Desire,
and the Art of Simple Cooking*

TREYF

TREYF

MY LIFE AS AN UNORTHODOX OUTLAW

ELISSA ALTMAN

OPEN ROAD
INTEGRATED MEDIA
NEW YORK

This is a memoir, which is an act of memory rather than history. The events and experiences rendered here are all true as the author has remembered them to the best of her ability, and as older stories were related to her over the years. Some names and circumstances have been changed in order to protect the privacy of individuals involved.

Cover and interior design by Susan Turner

ISBN: 978-1-5040-9356-9

This edition published in 2024 by Open Road Integrated Media, Inc.
180 Maiden Lane
New York, NY 10038
www.openroadmedia.com

*For all those who came before and helped guide the way,
and for Susan, my heart and home.*

CONTENTS

PART III

TREYF

PROLOGUE

F *LEISHIG OR MILCHIG?"*
 It is 1995.

A middle-aged Hasidic antiques dealer on Second Avenue opens a splintering mahogany box and removes a tarnished silver serving set: a knife, a fork, a spoon.

We stand face-to-face in our respective uniforms: me, in paisley Doc Martens boots and a pilling, mauve Benetton sweater with rounded shoulder pads that make me look a fullback. He, in sober black pants, black vest, black shoes, black suede yarmulke, and a white-on-white chain-patterned shirt stained with the sweat of devotion, his tzitzit—the fringes of his prayer shawl—dangling beneath his fingers. A plume of graying black hair cascades up and out of his collar.

"It's very nice," he says, holding the fork up to the light streaming in through the windows, "but I see this pattern a lot. It's from the Kennedys."

. . .

AFTER DATING FOR FIVE MONTHS, my parents married in 1962. My father was sure he had found the love of his life, and his future; my mother was sure she had found a way out of her parents' house, and her future.

They were both right, and they were both wrong.

I was born nine months later, almost to the day. My father tells me this story for years, from the time I am old enough to understand what the words mean, and probably even before: that I was conceived on their wedding night, hours after their ceremony was presided over by Rabbi Charles Kahane—father of Jewish Defense League founder and crackpot firebrand Meir, murdered in 1990—and the kosher reception held at Terrace on the Park, overlooking the sinkhole that was Flushing Meadows, site of the World's Fair two years later.

"It all happened very fast," my father explains.

BEFORE HE MARRIED MY MOTHER, my father was engaged five times, each time to a woman his family deemed unacceptable.

"Treyf," his mother said to me as she recounted the story, tipping her chin in the air and rolling her eyes: one was too big, another too short, another cross-eyed, another crazy, another not Jewish.

Treyf: According to Leviticus, *unkosher and prohibited*, like lobster, shrimp, pork, fish without scales, the mixing of meat and dairy. But also, according to my grandmother, *imperfect, intolerable, offensive, undesirable, unclean, improper, filthy, broken, forbidden, illicit, rule-breaking*.

A person can eat treyf; a person can be treyf.

"And then," my grandmother said, "he met your mother."

She folded her arms across her ample breast and heaved a long sigh.

My mother.

My tall, blond, fur model, television singer mother who I watched men trip over themselves to get to at the 1960s and 1970s Queens, New York, parties of my childhood.

When she met my father, a sack-suited, wing-tipped ad man specializing in postwar Long Island real estate, she had recently ended a relationship with the composer Bernie Wayne. Somewhere between Bernie and my father, there was someone I will call Thomas, a tall, Jewish, French-speaking, Sorbonne-educated beatnik who had purportedly once lived with Nina Simone, and whose diamond-dealer father had been knighted by the king of Belgium. When I was ten, my parents brought me along to one of Thomas's legendary Saturday night Upper East Side cocktail parties, where I careened around the crowded apartment from table to table like a pinball, narrowly dodging the suede-patched elbows and lit Gitanes of the other guests. Invisible and unsupervised, I managed, just as the party was getting underway, to eat an entire block of pâté de campagne, a bowl of cornichons, and a round of stinking, oozing Époisses. An hour later, I writhed on Thomas's bathroom floor like a snake and was comforted by some of the other guests while my parents went to get the car: the *Hollywood Squares* comedian David Brenner, who lived across the hall, rubbed my back; two prostitutes wearing matching black vinyl thigh-high platform boots and crushed purple velvet hot pants sang me a folk song accompanied by a cheap nylon-string guitar that one of them had brought along; and a long-haired man who claimed to be the drummer for Chicago scratched my head like I was a puppy. Forty years later, I can see the black-and-white octagonal tiles on Thomas's bathroom floor, and I can feel the stiff nylon weave of the polyester shag rug burning my neck.

"*Treyf*," my mother's mother, Gaga, whispered to me as she mopped my forehead the next morning, while my parents slept soundly in their bedroom across the hall.

AFTER THEIR WEDDING CEREMONY, after the blessings were made by my paternal Grandpa Henry, a fire-and-brimstone Orthodox cantor, after the chopped liver was eaten, the gefilte loaf sliced, the Manischewitz Heavy Malaga poured and the hora danced, my parents drove to their honeymoon at the most modern of the upstate New York kosher borscht belt hotels, the Nevele, with their silver serving set locked in the trunk of their rental car. They had made it; they were finally legitimate. They had stepped on the glass, jumped the broom, leapt the chasm between freedom and conformity, adolescence and adulthood; they had done exactly what was expected of them.

Every member of my father's family had the same set of silver—a Gorham service in the Etruscan Greek Key pattern—as if it was a shining periapt acknowledging their validity and confirming their eternal place in the clan. As a young child, I was regularly seated on a beige vinyl kitchen stool near the sink, while Gaga methodically polished the pieces; the process hypnotized me, and I watched without blinking how she tied a silk paisley kerchief around her nose and mouth like a bandit on *Bonanza*, poured the thick, pink Noxon onto a soft rag and massaged each utensil until it shone, silver and glowing and bright as a pearl. I was mesmerized by the pattern's simplicity and would hold the tarnished spoon on my lap and trace the design with my tiny index finger: it was nothing more than a straight line that flowed forward, then reticently coiled back on itself. It turned and moved forward again, repeating over and over without end. My father's family didn't arrive at Ellis Island from the old country with a family crest, and so we adopted the Greek Key as our own; it became ubiquitous, gracing everything from the edges of our linen tablecloths to our bath towels to the border around the hood of the English Balmoral pram my parents pushed me around the Upper East Side in when I was an infant.

A gift to my parents from my father's sister and her husband and his sisters—Gaga called them *fancy people*; there was no love lost in either direction—the family silver bore witness to every tribal event that took place in our home from the early 1960s into the 1970s: tense Mother's Day brunches and prim Thanksgivings. Funeral luncheons and birthday parties crackling with rage. It graced a decade of sweet Rosh Hashanah tables, prawnfilled cocktail parties, solemn shivas when well-meaning Catholic neighbors carried in trays of cheese-stuffed shells floating in meat sauce; holiday parties where bacon-wrapped water chestnuts and party franks were served with potato latkes; and Yom Kippur break fasts where we set upon platters of sable and lox like a drowning man grabs for a life preserver.

When the parties were over, the only things remaining were invisible coils of gossip, and the ancient family furies—the confidences breached, the grudges held, the forbidden flaunted and waved like a victory flag—that were spoken of in hushed tones and hung in the air like crepe paper streamers. Gaga waited until the last guest departed, plunked me down on the stool next to her, dumped the silver into the sink, and I watched in silence as she scoured away any trace of what had been eaten and what had been whispered, rendering it perfect and clean and kosher for the next occasion.

"So *nu*," the Hasidic antiques dealer says to me again, pushing his black plastic glasses up the bridge of his nose: "Do you know? Fleishig or milchig?"

Meat or dairy?

If I can assure him that the silver had been used in a devout home, where separate sets of plates and silverware are restricted for dairy and meat dishes, he won't have to go to the trouble of koshering it for a Jewish customer wanting to buy it. He won't have to put the set through the lengthy process of *hag'alah*—boiling the pieces while keeping them from touching each other so that every bit of the silver is exposed to the cleansing promise of the water, like baptism in a river.

I don't know what to say, given all the years of meat lasagnas and pork dumplings and shrimp cocktails that the silver has served during my parents' ill-fated marriage. After sixteen years, their relationship ended in the late 1970s, not in a modern Manhattan divorce court like in *Kramer vs. Kramer*, but in front of a *beth din*—a quorum of three Orthodox rabbis—who agreed, after some Talmudic debate, to grant them a *get*, a kosher document of marriage severance from husband to wife dating back to the days of Deuteronomy, and without which even the most assimilated Jewish couple, having gone through an American divorce court, is still considered married according to Talmudic law.

"AHA," he gasps, holding up the knife, flecked with a tiny, hardened drop of dark red jam. He removes his glasses, holds his jeweler's loop up to his eye, and confirms it with a combination of Talmudic reasoning and authority: "We don't eat jam unless it's with blintzes and blintzes are dairy. Therefore," he proclaims triumphantly, "milchig!"

The last time I saw my parents' silver serving pieces in use was when I was ten, the night of my father's fiftieth birthday in 1973 during an ice storm—*the* ice storm; the Rick Moody–Ang Lee ice storm when New York nearly came to a standstill—when the delivery boy from the local deli couldn't get his truck up the street to drop off the trays of food that my mother had ordered for what was supposed to be a grand surprise party. It was a bust; there was nothing to eat. Grandpa Henry called just as we were all starting to hide behind my parents' black silk couch, and I jumped up to answer the phone. My father walked in, exhausted, his Harris tweed overcoat caked with melting slush, his woolen driver's cap wet and dripping, and everyone yelled *Surprise!* and my grandfather said that he wouldn't be there because it was the Sabbath.

"Tell him for me I'm sorry, Elissala dahlink," he mumbled in his thick Yiddish accent, and then he hung up.

"He always goes to all your sister's parties," my mother snarled, "whether it's Shabbos or not." She pulled him into their bedroom where they fought behind closed doors while the hungry neighbors downed glasses of scotch and I raided the fridge and produced a beige melamine platter of overlapping sliced salami, intermarrying the Oscar Mayer with the Hebrew National like a Unitarian Venn diagram. I put it out with a jar of Gulden's mustard and half a loaf of my mother's crumbling Pepperidge Farm diet white bread that I judiciously sliced into points, the way I had once watched Julia Child do on television. With no sign of the deli boy, the neighbors left and returned with whatever they could exhume from their refrigerators and cupboards: Polly from across the hall made Jell-O salad with cubed lemon-flavored Brach's marshmallow Easter bunnies unearthed from the bowels of her candy cabinet. Carole from two flights up defrosted a pound of chopped meat under a waterfall of steaming bathwater and made Swedish meatballs with a container of milk she procured from the vending machine in the basement. My mother's best friend, Inga, came back with a small boneless ham that she had basted with glaze under high heat until it resembled an overgrown Halloween candy apple. By seven o'clock, I pressed my ear to my parents' bedroom door, and the shouting had slowed—they were spent and exhausted—while my father's boss was on his fifth Dewar's and playing my little wooden bongo drums in the living room while freezing rain pelted our windows. Wearing a fez and with his shirt unbuttoned to his navel like Tom Jones, my father's best friend, Buck, hacked at the ham's candy coating with the tip of the silver knife while Harry Belafonte's "Jumbie Jamberee" played in the background. We all gathered around while my father sliced his birthday cake, which was decorated like the real estate advertising pages of the *New York Times* and had been sitting on our terrace in the December cold for the better part of a week.

Twenty-two years later, I stare out the window of the antique shop, watching the traffic barrel down Second Avenue. I can taste the gummy Swedish meatballs thick with curdled milk and the Easter bunny marshmallows in the Jell-O salad. I can smell Buck's Paco Rabanne, and see him in his Glen plaid Sansabelt trousers, chipping away at Inga's candy apple ham. The antique dealer will never know that the little speck on my parents' wedding silver set is not jam, but a stray bit of petrified pork glaze, hardened when my parents were still married and Nixon was still in office.

MY FATHER LIBERATED THE SILVER set from my mother right before their divorce, before she had a chance to change the locks; he kept it for me for fourteen years, hidden away deep in his mother's walkin closet in Coney Island, next to an ancient bottle of Slivovitz and a shopping bag stuffed with photos of long-dead cousins from the old country, taken right before the Nazis marched in. "So you just took it?" I asked, when he guiltily came clean about it one Saturday when I was sixteen, during his parental weekend visitation. We were having dinner at The Praha Restaurant in Manhattan, and he was nursing his second Gibson and poking at a plate of warm, apricot-stuffed palascinta. It was a bitterly cold night; ice rimed the windows like a frozen beer mug.

"She'd hock it if I didn't—" he said, his eyes red and pleading, "and then you'd never know who you are. I'm keeping it safe and sound until you get married; then, it's yours."

After I lied for years whenever my mother went on a tear about her missing silver serving pieces—You know, don't you? she'd say to me; "You know that he stole them, you're protecting him," her brown eyes fierce with rage—my father handed it over to me unceremoniously when I turned thirty after I told him I preferred women to men.

"No use in waiting anymore, then," he said wistfully, stroking the mahogany case. He turned and walked out, leaving me standing alone in the middle of my tiny studio apartment, cradling the purloined box in my arms like an infant. The premarital giving of the family silver set marked me both as an adult, the family's most ardent rule-breaker, and the family's certain failure; I would never marry a man, and the traditional handoff on my assumed wedding day—what I was taught as a child would be a big affair at a country club on Long Island with a tall white multitiered cake and my Aunt Sylvia dancing a Russian sher—would never happen.

"Who do you think you are, to cheat us out of joy, to break the chain?" Aunt Sylvia whispered to me quietly in her kitchen the Thanksgiving after I came out, when I helped carry in plates from her table.

"I don't know," I said And I didn't.

I had no idea who I was.

For almost two years, the silver pieces sat hidden and covered in a blanket of thick dust on the bottom shelf of my television armoire, tucked behind a stack of ancient VHS tapes. I opened it only on Yom Kippur, the Jewish Day of Atonement, when WQXR's simulcast of the Kol Nidre services from Manhattan's Temple Emanuel at sundown. The cantor chanted and I opened the box and released an angry Pandora: a musty, acrid pong rushed out of it like a wave and wrapped itself around me. The smell of the past—a gamey, trans-portive scent of despair and schmaltz and Aqua Net—made me woozy. I'd close the lid quickly and put the box back where I'd hid-den it, complicit in my father's pilfering, and where my mother would never find it.

The Greek Key signified our wandering path, our twisting course, our constant searching and moving forward while always turning back. It was a pattern of repetition; a tether to the past.

"Without it," my father warned when he handed it over, "you'll never know who you are."

PART I

He speaks in your voice, American,
and there's a shine in his eye that's
halfway hopeful.

—Don DeLillo, *Underworld*

1

The Kitchen

A HUNDRED AND FIFTY POUNDS. Maybe closer to two." *Two hundred pounds?*

The phone is tucked between my ear and my shoulder; I am feeding the dog. There's silence. The man on the other end of the phone coughs.

"Look," he tells me. "You ordered half a pig. They're animals. We can't predict."

I am standing in the center of the cluttered kitchen in my early-1970s ranch house in a bucolic part of Connecticut, now famous for its gun violence and its beauty. I move the phone to my other ear and wash out the dog bowls. A mundane, ordinary activity—feeding the dog; talking on the phone—but it starts when I least expect it; it hasn't happened for years. Out of nowhere, my heart begins to pound and slam against the inside of my chest; it's late autumn, and although we keep the house at a cool sixty-six degrees, my back is sticky with a thin layer of sweat. I put the bowls down in the sink and grab the kitchen towel from where it hangs off the refrigerator handle; I drag it across my forehead. Breathe and hold; breathe and hold. My pulse slows, and I look around the kitchen; I need to make sure that it's really there, that I'm really standing on my own two adult feet, in it. A smell, a picture, an inherited dinner plate, a piece of gefilte fish, can send me hurtling backwards, ass over elbow, to a place and time where I observed rather than lived, where safety was an illusion. I belong here—with my wife, our dog, our house in New England; I've worked so hard to get here, to this place of calm and peace, where my life and my beliefs are my own—but I'm from there. And there is where it starts.

IT'S EARLY EVENING, OCTOBER, DUSKY; I haven't turned on the school-house lights over the island, and so everything around me is wrapped in a gray, muddled cast, like a dream. The kitchen hypnotizes and grounds me, and I gape with wonder at this space, filled with life and history and sustenance.

Here, in the physical center of the house I share with my wife of fifteen years, there's a Viking six-burner stove—it has old-fashioned dials and knobs, not the fancy digital dashboard that the salesman tried to convince us to buy; the words BAKE and BROIL have melted with time—sandwiched against a heavily used, stained yellow laminate countertop that wraps around a matching chipped yellow sink and a single-arm faucet stiff with years of lime buildup, set on top of birch veneer site-built cabinets that we painted white eight years ago. A crank-arm casement window looks out over the backyard to where our vegetable garden was planted and cultivated before we expanded it to six boxes from four, and moved it to the front of the house. A harvest calendar dangles from a magnetic hook attached to the side of the stainless-steel refrigerator; a cherry console table sagging under the weight of a stand mixer and a massive English ceramic mortar and pestle is propped under a wall-mounted, hand-hewn iron pot rack given to us by a famous French chef from Manhattan; it is laden with stainless sauté pans blackened with years of use.

A pile of jet-black cast-iron Griswold pans, inherited from Susan's Aunt Ethel, is stacked up on the shelf under the island. An old cream-colored, glass-front cupboard that I bought years ago from a Westport consignment shop leans against one wall, packed with two dozen ironstone platters crazed with time; a smaller, walnut cupboard, which sat in my paternal grandmother's Coney Island kitchen for almost seventy years and for decades gave off small clouds of chicken fat every time its doors were opened, is filled with hundreds of spice canisters. After my grandmother died in the early 1990s, her daughter, my Aunt Sylvia, took possession of the fragrant cabinet; she had it refinished a mossy army green, the color of the dangerous forest in a Grimm's fairy tale, and used it to hold the delicate flowered porcelain tea service that her own grandmother carried over from Romania in 1893. Eventually, Sylvia tired of the cupboard and passed it along to her daughter, Lois, who refinished it again, stood it in a darkened corner of her Long Island home near her powder room and used it to store twenty-five Passover Haggadahs and her physician husband's collection of vintage white china invalid feeders. After a few years, Lois didn't want it either, but needing to keep it in the family, she passed it along to me.

There was no question that I'd take it; of course I would, even though I didn't much like it any more than anyone else did. It was like a particularly hideous piece of heirloom jewelry that everyone fawned over when it hung from the neck of its owner, but secretly loathed. Nobody wanted the cupboard, but nobody would dare turn it down either, or break the family chain, as if saying no was tantamount to rejection of our bloodline and our history. It's lived for years in my kitchen—longer than at Lois's house, and longer than at Aunt Sylvia's. I've made it mine; it's unrecognizable now, with new pulls and its Napoleonic finial unscrewed, removed, and long discarded; it's filled now with the stuff of comfort—glass canisters holding everything from Lebanese za'atar to hot pimentón and dried heirloom Chimayo chiles and brown mustard seed from India. On top of it is perched a copper stockpot from Dehillerin in Paris and a black clay soup tureen from Colombia. My grandmother's cupboard, which was passed from home to home out of duty, has landed here, where it is cherished; I can do nothing but smile every time I look at it. What had long been an albatross of obligation, the cupboard has become a kitchen witness, a repository of nourishment and life.

This is my sanctuary, my refuge, my safe room; when Susan and I bought this otherwise unremarkable ranch house twelve years ago, in 2004, we did so because the kitchen sits at its center. It's unavoidable and inescapable and the physical heart of our home. Meals are made here; rules are broken here; new traditions have begun here.

"I'll come on Friday," I tell the man on the phone, stirring a tablespoon of canned pumpkin into our ancient Labrador's kibble. I toss in an anti-inflammatory for Addie's groaning hips and prednisone for her allergies and set it down in front of her. It's gone, Hoovered up like a dust bunny before I turn around. My panic has receded; it's just another day.

"Come on Friday," he repeats. "Three o'clock, so we have time to process and package everything."

"Okay," I say, "three o'clock." And then I hang up.

Two hours up to western Massachusetts, two hours back. I drive my old red Forester through the lower Berkshire hills at the height of leaf season; it's late fall, and I fight meandering buses full of fanny-packed leaf peepers as I head north up Route 8 through Torrington and into what had been the industrial mill town of Winsted, now a jumble of small antique shops and churches and a Goodwill. I pass through quiet, rolling Norfolk, where Yale holds its summertime classical music series, and over the Massachusetts border into Sheffield, where the road widens to a broad ribbon of dove gray nestled amidst a sudden, abrupt, nearly hysterical burst of explosive color. This is New England in autumn, a time of year that has been immortalized in calendar photographs and on L.L. Bean catalog covers; it's what everyone thinks of when they think of this part of the world. It's bucolic, American, Waspy, comfortable, predictable. It has become my home.

I have folded down the backseat and packed the car with six coolers of varying sizes: Susan's late father's red and white plastic

Coleman cooler from the early 1960s is shoved between two softs-ided insulated bags. Massive Styrofoam beer coolers are nestled into each other like Russian dolls, and Susan has thought to line the cargo tray with black plastic industrial contractor bags in case of leakage. Twenty miles into western Massachusetts, not far from Stockbridge where, in six weeks, like the song says, the first of December will be covered with snow, I pull into a gravel driveway that curls around to the side of a cavernous, red-painted barn, a silver silo, and a small, ominous-looking cinder block building whose wood-burning stove is belching plumes of white, fatty smoke into the air. The place belongs to the man I talked to—a middle-aged, beer-bellied butcher wearing stained, caramel-colored Carhartt overalls and a red woolen cap. He's old-school, the best, everyone has told me. He opens the back hatch of my car and packs my coolers with bags of ice and half a custom-butchered Tamworth hog: giant cuts of fresh ham and butt for the Christmas holidays, two dozen three-pound blocks of fatty, boneless pork belly, baby back ribs, country-style ribs, a standing rib roast, chops, cubed stew meat, four shanks, four trotters, two ears, and a tail.

"Everything but the squeal," he says through a yellowing mustache, wiping his hands on his pants.

I hand him a check; he squints at it, folds it up, shoves it in the breast pocket of his coveralls, shakes my hand, and I leave for home with roughly two hundred pounds of heirloom pork in the back of my car.

I weave my way back south through the hills; I take the rural route, avoiding the towns, and consider what I will make for dinner, given the beast—a nod to food trend and excess more than to need; no couple actually needs half an adult pig—that I'm carrying home to my kitchen. The sun begins to set slowly and I remember that it is Shabbos, and the prayer I spoke nearly every Friday night during my childhood summers echoes in my head—it's been forty years since I learned it—and I whisper it to myself:

Thy Sabbath has come.

2

The Year of the Mitzvah

O N A SUNNY SATURDAY MORNING in the late spring of 1974, Candy Feinblatt became a woman.

She stood on the gold-carpeted bimah in front of friends and family at the Forest Hills Jewish Center, her long, deep-parted sun-dappled blond hair cascading forward, hippie-style, over her shoulders and down to her waist. On that day, with Nixon not yet out of office and The Streak blaring out of open car windows cruising up and down Queens Boulevard, my best friend was called to the Torah dressed in a special bat mitzvah outfit chosen by her mother: a blue-and-red-flecked Huk-A-Poo blouse, black peep-toe Carber sandals, and a tan suede miniskirt under which she wore suntan panty hose. Candy's tomboy days of stiff, rolled-up Wranglers and flannel shirts were officially over; I was on my own.

Candy, suddenly statuesque in her wedges, chanted in perfect phonetic Hebrew, holding the heavily ornate silver yad—the pointer; touching the Torah is considered ritual defilement under Jewish law—in her right hand. She chewed nervously on her lower lip when she lost her place in the scroll; the cantor, his face beet red from the heat, sidled up to her and offered help, his soft brown kiltie loafers squeaking as though they'd been soaked in water. Everything that day was damp with humidity: the pages of my prayer book, the scalp beneath my blond frizzy afro, the armpits of my tight rayon blouse and the entire lower half of my body, which was encased like a salami in a narrow ladies' denim maxi skirt festooned with butterfly applique and dime-sized silver studs, bought for me by my mother at her favorite boutique and hemmed eight inches by our local tailor before I could wear it. It was a point of pride that once I hit eleven years old, she bought all of my outfits where she bought her own; my friends were still wearing clothes purchased for them by their parents in the kids' department at Bloomingdale's and Macy's, while I was dressed up like a smaller version of my 1970s New York City mother, in long skirts and transparent voile blouses and elasticized tube tops that clung precariously to my suggestion of a chest.

When Candy finished her haftorah and everyone mumbled amen, she looked out from her place on the bimah and scanned the congregation. We all stared back in silent awe. Her mother, Marion, sat in the first pew, directly in front of me and my parents and Gaga; she wore a flat-topped chapeau bedecked with pastel flowers and more suitable for a Mississippi funeral than a bat mitzvah in Queens. Candy's father, Eugene, president of the synagogue, sat behind his daughter up on the bimah, perched on an immense oak and burgundy velvet throne. He uncoiled his tall lanky frame, stood up, loped over to give his daughter a hug and nervously patted the royal blue crushed velvet yarmulke bobbypinned to his jet-black combover.

Rabbi Schneiderman clapped Eugene hard on the back, and then put his hands on Candy's narrow shoulders.

"Today, Candy," bellowed the rabbi, "you have become an adult in the eyes of this community, your friends, and your family. You are a woman now, and you will be expected to carry out the rules and commandments handed down to the people Israel from Hashem, Blessed Be He, all the days of your life."

He kissed Candy on both cheeks. She stood stiffly, her hands dangling by her sides like a ragdoll, and then floated down from the bimah to sit next to Marion, who was quietly weeping with pride.

"Now," announced Rabbi Schneiderman, "the Feinblatt family would like to extend a cordial invitation to join them in a luncheon in honor of their young lady, directly across the street at the Tung Shing House. Please join us first in the oneg room for coffee and tea. Thank you all for coming, and Gut Shabbos." It was May, and the shul was stifling; beads of sweat dotted my father's brow as we stood to leave the sanctuary. He pulled at his gold paisley tie to loosen the wide Windsor knot and when we stepped out into the lobby, he removed his prayer shawl—striped in white and blue and darkly yellowed around the neck from his boyhood days in a hot Brooklyn synagogue while his cantor father led one hundred clinically depressed Orthodox immigrants in ancient prayer—and tucked it into its blue velvet pouch. He zipped it closed and stepped outside for a cigarette.

"Are we going to the oneg?" I asked my mother, following her into the bathroom where she began to reapply her makeup, which the humidity had melted during the service. Black eyeliner dripped down her face as though she had been crying. "It's just the heat," she sighed to another woman who gently touched her arm with concern.

"You go ahead—I'll meet you downstairs. Gaga is already there," my mother said to my reflection in the mirror while she rifled around in her suede fringed purse. She pulled out my black rubber afro pick and handed it to me.

"Fix your hair before you go outside—just a little touch-up." I scowled and gave it back to her.

"There might be a boy, honey. You always have to be ready—" I ran the pick over my head, left it on the edge of the sink, and went to look for Candy, who I found standing in front of a dented silver coffee urn with a black spigot, surrounded by a throng of well-wishers as though she had just been married.

• • •

MY FATHER USED TO SAY that you could always tell a Jewish neighborhood by the location of its Chinese restaurant.

The Tung Shing House sat at the very heart of our town, at the convergence of two major arteries: overcrowded, congested Yellowstone Boulevard and the pulsing, aortic Queens Boulevard, the eight-lane thoroughfare of doom that split Forest Hills in half from east to west and connected travelers to glamorous Manhattan on one end and opulent Long Island on the other, assuming they weren't killed along the way. The boulevard was infamous for its number of monthly vehicular deaths so regular that local dress shops kept extra bolts of cheap fabric on hand for covering up the bodies until the ambulances could arrive.

The Tung Shing House stood in the middle of Forest Hills like a bull's-eye and was the site of feasts large and small, celebratory and mundane; walk in on any given Saturday, and you might be interrupting a bat mitzvah luncheon like Candy's. Walk in on a Sunday night, and every Jewish family in town, mine included, was lined up, waiting to order platters of shrimp in lobster sauce.

At the end of every weekend, my parents and I would gather up Gaga and stroll the half mile down Austin Street and around the corner onto Yellowstone, past my junior high school, which, in the early 1970s had become newsworthy for the regular fights that took place in the second floor girls' bathroom, and for Mr. Nedling, the school's quaalude-addled gym teacher who had a history of looking the other way just as his students sailed over the pummel horse. Every Sunday night, we stood for an hour in the restaurant foyer, waiting for a table, scanning the three-columned menu handed to us by the same brusque Chinese waiter wearing a short gold jacket with black brocade epaulets. And every Sunday night, we ordered the same things: the Polynesian pupu platter—sticky, ruby red–glazed spareribs, fried dumplings, steamed dumplings, fried egg rolls, fried shrimp toast—delivered to our table on a black enameled Lazy Susan, the dishes arranged around a live blue alcohol flame that emitted a kerosene stink and utterly terrorized me. There were heavy bowls of salty, MSG-infused wonton soup laden with flaccid, dark green bok choy that floated on the surface like sea kelp; there was Gaga's favorite chicken chow mein, thick with clear glop, and into which she stirred half a cup of soy sauce; mucusy shrimp in lobster sauce that my father loved and shoveled onto great piles of burnished fried rice speckled with tiny cubes of red meat the color of blood.

During those Sunday suppers in our local Chinese restaurant, my father ate silently, carnally, hunched over his bowl of soup dumplings stuffed with meat of unknown provenance; my mother poked tentatively at the segregated piles on her plate while he gnawed on the crimson spareribs like a hyena after a kill, the glaze smearing his lips and cheeks until all that was left were the bare bones. He ate like a starving, voracious child, ravenous with hunger and need, never once looking up or stopping to breathe until his plate was clean. It fascinated and thrilled me; I loved the fanfare, the otherwise forbidden eating with our hands, the tearing of meat from bone, and the belly-patting grunts that my father emitted as he paid the bill and we stood to leave, running into other Jewish neighbors waiting for our table to open up when we stepped outside.

"IS THIS CHICKEN?" I asked my father at Candy's bat mitzvah luncheon, as the waiter dropped a pot overflowing with tea between us. I pointed at the familiar, narrow shred of meat on my porcelain soup spoon. It was gray and tipped with a bright red splotch, like a matchstick.

"Just eat it," he murmured quietly, and slurped his soup while his black plastic aviators fogged up.

"Is it?" I asked again, my voice getting whiney and high. I tapped my spoon on my water glass. Then I tapped my bowl and then my water glass and then my mother's wineglass, which she moved to the other side of her plate. I wanted my father's attention, but I didn't want to go overboard; if I accidentally spilled my mother's wine, I'd spend the rest of the meal banished to the damp tile floor of the restaurant basement, which housed the ladies' and men's bathrooms and an old black payphone hanging from the wall, and where a cloud of industrial cleaners and ammonia overtook the smell of frying egg rolls and chow mein. If I misbehaved at the table, this is where I would wind up, memorizing the tile pattern and waiting until my father came back downstairs to get me.

"Not now," my father repeated through clenched teeth. He frowned at me over the top of his glasses and sucked the greens off his spoon. "Just eat your soup."

"But—" I said, tapping my bowl harder.

"EAT YOUR SOUP, dammit—"

"BUT—"

"I will tell you later," my father growled, shoving a bowl of crunchy fried noodles at me while my mother and Gaga watched, silently.

So I ate. And so did my father and Gaga and my mother, who delicately dipped the tip of a crunchy noodle into the little wooden dish of duck sauce and then into mustard before nibbling at it like a gerbil. All of Candy's family and other friends slurped away, chattering, unconcerned about the contents of their bowls. Twerpy Marcus Goldberg, who, at twelve, wore a too-small hand-me-down madras blazer that choked his armpits and who only came up to the underside of my recently acquired bosom; Lisa Epstein, whose mother made her walk around their apartment balancing books on her head so that she could become a Ford model; damp-handed Stuart Steinman, who at nine had sprouted the beginnings of a mustache and by eleven was trying to nail any girl with a pulse: all of us, our parents, and the Feinblatts gorged that day without any concern about what they were eating. It would be years before I learned that the Chinese soup dumplings my father had told me were identical to the kreplach that his mother often fed me on our trips to Brooklyn were actually stuffed with ground pork and scallions, and the red-tipped gray meat bobbing beneath the soup greens were the restaurant's leftovers from hong shao rou—barbecued pork—that every Cantonese-style commercial kitchen roasted by the truckload.

NINETEEN SEVENTY-FOUR WAS THE YEAR of the Mitzvah, Bar and Bat. Three years before Son of Sam terrorized our neighborhood and

Candy lost her virginity to a boy named Pedro, 1974 would be a cease-less string of celebrations that ran the gamut from joyful to mawkish, eccentric to staid. Suddenly, every one of my friends was being called to the bimah; even my not-so-religious friends paid the altar an abridged visit, like the *Reader's Digest* version, while I watched along-side my parents in synagogues all over Queens. Even my half-Jewish friends like Neil Taub, whose mother was a French-Canadian Catho-lic with a tiny windup porcelain model of a bug-eyed Singing Nun that twirled in circles like a dervish on her nightstand while playing Domi-nique—even they were bar mitzvahed.

For the devout, like the Feinblatts, there were Tung Shing House luncheons that followed long, formal religious ceremonies. For the less pious, there were truncated services that took place everywhere from vinyl slip–covered living rooms overlooking the Grand Central Parkway to the Oasis Middle Eastern Restaurant, where a stout, hir-sute belly dancer with a plastic sapphire in her navel left the boys in my class panting with lust. These more secular events were often punctuated by bowling parties at Hollywood Lanes, softball games in nearby Kissena Park, and in my case, a clown named Sid, at the Spaghetti Factoria in Manhattan, on Fifty-Ninth Street just off Madison Avenue.

A year earlier, with the low hum of prepubescent, tone-deaf prayer overtaking our apartment building and all of my friends disappearing from our afternoon handball courts and playgrounds in order to cram for their ceremonies, I announced to my father that I wanted to join them as they embarked on their journey to man- and womanhood. I was feeling left out. I wanted to go to Hebrew school, too.

We weren't particularly practicing Jews, so my sudden compulsion could have been purely environmental, and the result of four hours spent glued to the television every Passover, watching Anne Baxter and Charlton Heston in The Ten Commandments, frolicking in the sands of the Sinai and leading his people to freedom with the help of tan, pouty-mouthed John Derek. After seeing it for the first time when I was four, I sashayed around our apartment wrapped in a bedsheet, pointed at our Schnauzer, Binky, and shouted, BEHOLD!

"Are we Levites, Daddy?" I chirped sweetly during a commercial break. "Like Joshua?"

"We're Altmans," he said, looking at me over the top of his National Geographic, "like the store."

In 1973, I suddenly lusted after piety and holiness the way a child lusts after a Christmas pony. On television, God-fearing people were always being depicted as being kind and loving and patient, and when Billy Graham marched across the stage shouting, GOD FORGIVES, GOD FORGIVES, I closed my bedroom door with shaking hands, locked it from the inside and watched him with longing and desire and a sort of alien burning heat that started somewhere around my navel; I turned the volume way down low, like it was porn.

"What the hell are you doing in there?" Gaga shouted, rattling the doorknob. Mishegas, I heard her mumble, before tromping down the hallway and into the kitchen.

Whoever they were, if they were on television and they were devout, I was addicted to them: the Waltons, who were drowning under the glorious weight of old-time mountain religion, which seemed to help them weather every storm from the Depression to Nazis to Ellen Corby's stroke. Eventually, I found my way to contemplative devotion in Kung Fu and watched the show every week, silent and gape-mouthed, as Grasshopper defused violence, racism, and anger without resorting to physical aggression. That had to be a nice religion.

"She's locked in her goddamn bedroom again, watching that Chinaman," Gaga complained to my mother in the hallway as she banged on my door. "Careful, or she'll join the Moonies."

I didn't care who or what they were: I yearned to join the team of the just and the right. I yearned to be forgiven for everything that I could possibly think of: For eating my dinner too fast. For not eating at all. For not being pretty enough. For failing math. For taunting the dog. For breaking a water glass. For not doing my homework. For not being perfect, like my cousins. For not liking boys. For not being grateful. For not being good.

One night I sat my father down after he came home from work and kicked off his cordovans onto his clothing butler: I wanted to make the officially sanctioned leap out of pubescence into adulthood, like Candy was going to. I wanted to find God in the way that she had since going to Hebrew school every week, blissed out and passionate and all aglow with piety and virtue, like an azure mood ring stuck on happy. Other kids sang Found a Peanut and Billy Don't Be a Hero on the camp bus; she sang Hatikvah, the Israeli national anthem, at the top of her lungs.

"I want," I announced to my father, "to go to Hebrew school." I paused with drama; he stared at me, blinking.

"I want," I said, "to become a woman."

He raked his hands through his thinning hair.

"For Christ's sake, Lissie," he said, reaching for the remote to switch on the bedroom television set, "we're not even religious."

"We're not, Daddy," I said sweetly, "but you are." Which was mostly true.

The religion of my childhood was mechanical and routine: we lit an electric menorah on Hanukah and ate matzo on Passover. Gaga, convinced that nonkosher meat would somehow kill us in our sleep, only shopped at the local kosher butcher. My mother never discussed being Jewish; she scoffed at anyone provincial enough to devote themselves to Talmudic dictums designed for people living five thousand years before Pucci and Ella Fitzgerald. My father's link to his religion was one of rules and regulations and violent thrashings brought down on his tender young head by my Orthodox cantor grandfather, who believed that corporal punishment against his son—forcefully applied for everything from giggling during services to kicking his feet against the back of the synagogue seats to misreading his Hebrew lessons—was simply God's will; to my father, the religion of his birth translated into rage, frustration, and betrayal. So how could he trust a God who would allow him to be beaten by the man he loved most in the world? What kind of God would allow that to happen? But even young, I recognized the primal yearning for spiritual connection on my father's face. The piles of Roman Vishniac books sitting on our marble coffee table depicting black-hatted old men shuffling through the dusty streets of some nameless, long-forgotten shtetl with the shadow of death and destruction in their phlegmy eyes brought him to his knees every time he glanced at them; those men could have been him.

"Don't look at me," he would bark at my mother after erupting into sobs of shame and need. She glanced at him nervously and he slammed his books closed, put the leash on the dog, and went out for a walk.

The stacks of liturgical albums—Moishe Oysher singing Kol Nidre and Jan Peerce's Passover leaning up against my father's teak Garrard turntable next to The Modern Jazz Quartet—brought him back to the days of his Brooklyn childhood, when he thirsted for a God he could love, who would love him back as the little boy he was, instead of one who seemed to betray him with every blow willed to his father by Hashem, Blessed Be He.

Twice a year, we left my mother at home and made the long drive out to the tepid, airless Coney Island shul where my grandfather carried the Torah down the center aisle while I watched from upstairs in the mechitza, the separate women's seating where, since the age of five, I had been forced to sit. Looking over the railing into the sparse sanctuary, I watched my grandfather glide past his congregation as if on air, his eyes swollen and streaming with tears of devotion that began to flow the minute the service began. My father always positioned himself on the aisle so that my grandfather could see that he was there, that he really was a dutiful son after all and deserving not just of his father's love, but God's; from above, I would watch him try to catch my grandfather's eye as he carried the Torah down the middle of the shul. Even from high above his seat, I could see my father's yearning and straining. He longed for my grandfather to simply reach forward—just reach forward—and touch his shoulder, to acknowledge him. But rapt in Kabbalist keening, his mournful chest-beating during the viduy—the litanies of confession recited on Yom Kippur—my grandfather floated past his son without seeing him, his eyes closed, lost in reverie.

My father sighed at my pleading. But on the following Sunday morning, he threw his Burberry trench coat over his pajamas and tossed the Sunday *New York Times* magazine crossword puzzle onto the backseat of the Buick so he would have something to do while he waited for me. We left my mother standing alone in the kitchen nursing a cup of Sanka and smoking her breakfast cigarette, and drove the mile to my first Sunday school Hebrew class at Young Israel of Kew Forest.

My teacher, Miss Kranowitz, was waifish and wide-eyed. She strode around the room decorated with crayon renderings of the Hebrew alphabet wearing knee-high white vinyl go-go boots, her honey blond hair piled up on her head like a Gibson girl, and trailing a cloud of Tabu eau de cologne that made my mouth hang open. She blinked purposefully, like she was sending Morse code; when she put her hand on my shoulder, I thought I'd pass out.

I sat down next to my friend Rudy, who I'd known since kindergarten. Rudy's parents had divorced a year earlier and his mother, a square-jawed Viennese Lutheran, had been forced by her Jewish ex-husband to agree that their son would be bar mitzvahed, even though the only exposure Rudy had to Judaism was Allan Sherman and The 2000 Year Old Man. Rudy had no idea what aleph and bet—the first two letters of the Hebrew alphabet—were, but if you asked him what he thought about God, he'd point to the sky and repeat Mel Brooks's punch line with a thick Yiddish accent: there's something bigger than Phil.

When Miss Kranowitz asked the class if we knew what day the Sabbath was, I remembered Mama Walton, and the way she always forced the children to wash behind their ears and put on their best clothes on the Sabbath because it was the Lord's Day. My arrogant, pious little hand shot up like a rocket.

"Sunday!" I exclaimed.

Miss Kranowitz winced, like she'd stepped on a small shard of glass in her bare feet.

Idiot, Rudy murmured.

I was not invited to return to class the following week: the school cited my small assimilation problem as the cause for my predictable failure to fully learn and comprehend the lessons of the Talmud.

So unlike Marcus Goldberg and Lisa Epstein, tidy and neat Candy Feinblatt and Rudy of the Lutheran mother, I did not become a sanctified member of my community, and I was not officially expected to carry out the rules and commandments handed down to the people Israel from Hashem, Blessed Be He, all the days of my life.

Instead, to mark the occasion of what would have been my bat mitzvah the following June, a month after Candy's, my father simply decided, like Mrs. Dalloway, to have a party: he hired a gleaming white Mercedes twenty-seater bus and a driver to shuttle me and my friends to the Spaghetti Factoria in Manhattan. There, after Sid the Clown finished his animal balloon shtick and our hands began to tremble from too much Fanta, we were invited to grab a plate and sidle up to the restaurant's wall of disposable aluminum foil chafing dishes, where we could marry any number of varieties of butter-laden noodles—linguine, fusilli, elbows, ziti, rigatoni, spaghetti—to a spicy or mild red sauce containing, respectively, thick links of fennel sausage and golfball-sized cheese-stuffed polpettone.

Remembering the glory of Candy's bat mitzvah platters at the Tung Shing House, I chose both.

That night, intoxicated by the promise of my ersatz coming-of-age, I slept soundly and dreamt of gorgeous Miss Kranowitz who, through a fragrant fog of garlic bread and Tabu, placed her hands on my shoulders, bent down, and whispered in my ear, "Congratulations, Elissa. Today you are a woman."

3

The Country

W<small>E LIVED</small> in a thirteen-story redbrick apartment building in Forest Hills, Queens, called The Marseilles, which in style, sensi-
bility, and aroma, bore no resemblance to the light-splashed city of the
same name. My mother's brief addiction to espadrilles was as close as
we would ever get to the South of France. Built in 1960 along with The
Brussels, its larger partner across the fractured cement courtyard, the
buildings boasted shared amenities that included The Fountainbleu
swimming pool, The Champs-Élysées Promenade—an aquamarine-
tinted, crumbling stone walkway that connected the two buildings—
and The Riviera Garden Terrace, a brown concrete sundeck dropped
onto the roof of one of the buildings' three attached single-story ga-
rages. At the height of rush hour, when all of the fathers who lived in
The Marseilles and The Brussels arrived home from work, invisible
plumes of car exhaust wafted up and out of the garage, dizzying the
sunbathers and forcing them to flee as the sun began to set.

Luxury in Every Detail, the original rental brochure promised; A
Lavish Builderamic Design! Suites styled in the Riviera Tradition of

Elegance and Spaciousness! Which is why my grandmother, Gaga, woke up one morning in 1960 and made the executive decision, without consulting my grandfather, Philip, to uproot my twenty-something mother, who was still living at home, and get out of Dodge.

"We're moving to the country," Gaga announced to my mother over breakfast, the family story goes. She opened the *Daily News* and pointed to the full-page real estate ad. "It's just like The Riviera."

"What about Daddy?" my mother asked. "What about Daddy?"

"Are we just leaving him here—?"

"He'll come home on Friday night, for Shabbos," Gaga said. My grandfather, a furniture store owner, often slept on a dusty Victorian-era kilim fainting couch in his back storage room next to a potbellied stove so that he could tend to the flock of homing pigeons he kept on the roof of the building; limiting his visits to Friday nights wouldn't, my grandmother believed, ruffle his feathers.

And just like that, my mother and grandmother packed them-selves up from the two-bedroom apartment on Grand Street in Wil-liamsburg where they had lived since before World War II, and headed west to a community just seven miles from Manhattan. For-est Hills was known for its restricted, Brigadoon-like planned village of Edwardian mansions just down the street from The Marseilles and The Brussels, called, simply, The Gardens. Three blocks north stood the magnificent, ivy-covered Westside Tennis Club, original home of the U.S. Open, which wouldn't, my parents used to say when I became fanatical about the sport in grade school, have peo-ple like us as members.

"But why can't we join?" I whined after watching Billie Jean King beat Bobby Riggs in 1973. "It's right down the street."

"You'll hit against the schoolyard wall, like everyone else," my father said.

Off my mother and grandmother went, just as Ebbets Field was being demolished, to a large, south-facing apartment that overlooked the Long Island Rail Road tracks and shook every time the train blew past. After they moved in, Gaga painted the walls and the ceiling and all the trim the same milky mocha color, which gave their rare visitors the sense that they were drowning inside a cheap cup of coffee.

My grandfather grudgingly came home on Friday nights as Gaga required. The trip took two subways and over an hour from the Bedford Avenue stop in Williamsburg through the length of Manhattan and out to the wilds of Queens. Every Shabbos, Grandpa Philip walked in just as Gaga was hastily lighting her candles, and sat down to a meal prepared with neither piety nor ceremony: there was bland chicken soup with a tangle of narrow egg noodles that my grandmother cooked in the bottom half of her glass stovetop coffee percolator. There were saltines. There was a plate of skinless soup chicken. When the meal was over, my grandfather pushed himself away from the table, lit up a Super Corona, and puffed it out the window towards the railroad tracks before going to sleep in his single bed on the other side of the nightstand that he shared with his wife, their yellow Big Ben Moonbeam alarm clock casting a ghostly glow on the ceiling as the trains rattled by. And every Saturday morning, he got up, got dressed in the high-collared brown woolen suit and old-fashioned wingtip boots he always wore, opened the living room window, and sliced a thick wedge of Limburger from the block sitting on the sill where Gaga demanded he keep it. He left for the week and took the subway back through Queens and Manhattan into Brooklyn, to open the furniture store for his devoted, largely Italian Catholic clientele. Asked by leaders of the local Williamsburg Hasidic community to shutter his store on Shabbos, he politely but resolutely declined; he was a man of the people and if the majority of his customers would be in church on Sunday, he would remain open for them on Saturday. Until he died when I was four years old, Grandpa Philip repeated his Shabbos ritual every Friday night: subway to Queens, dinner, cigar, sleep, Limburger, leave.

My mother lived in that apartment for two years, commuting by subway to her modeling and singing gigs in Manhattan, coming home to sleep in my grandfather's single bed when he wasn't there, and on a dark gray chenille pull-out sofa in the living room when he was, like a guest.

. . .

"I HAD to get out of the house," my mother tells me years later, "so I married your father."

She snaps closed the silver Tiffany compact I gave her on her birthday twenty years earlier, in the 1990s; we're sitting at her favorite bistro in Manhattan, surrounded by gleaming white subway tiles and mirrors bearing the gray scuffs of intentional Frenchness. The bar, a few feet away, is a throng of drinkers sipping martinis: artists, writers, attorneys, brokers. The women are all the same color blond; their hair is all the same length and cut in the same style. They're all exactly the same height: tall. The place exudes beauty and glamour and a certain kind of effortless chic; it is everything my mother has strived for since she was a child and in love with movies and fashion, and achieved.

I've begun peppering her with questions about her marriage to my father, about when they met, and how, and under what circumstances. My father, on our weekends alone after the divorce, told me his version when I was an older teenager; I'd never heard hers and I wanted to—I wanted to know what it was that drew her to him and kept them together for sixteen acrimonious years of constant, relentless fighting. Was it the Talmudic promise of marriage? Was it lust?

My father, when we were on one of our many weekend getaways back when I was in college, mentioned taking her to a party filled with advertising executives on their first date.

"That's right," she says, nodding her head, dismantling the insides of a sourdough roll. "And then he borrowed ten dollars from me for a taxi to take me home to Forest Hills, because he was out of cash. I should have known right then and there. I should have known the way women know about these things."

She sighs and shakes her head dramatically.

To hear him tell the story, it was a different date: he did bring her to a party in Greenwich Village, packed with fancy Doyle Dane Bernbach executives whose success in the early 1960s had just bought them a new Upper East Side apartment, or a house on Long Island, or a Jaguar. Three of them knew her.

"Good luck," they said to my father, when his date went off to the ladies' room.

"I sent her a tiny gold pinky ring the next day, from the family jeweler," my father tells me.

"After your first date? Why? What did she do to deserve that?" I say, immediately regretting my question.

It comes out: my father was short on cash, and he couldn't take her home to Queens, which she expected him to do. There were no ATMs in those days, so he had to wait until Monday, when the banks reopened. He ran over to the jewelry district on his lunch hour, bought the ring, rolled up a ten like a joint, stuck the ring on it as if it was a finger, and messengered it off to the showroom where my mother was modeling furs.

"He was creative," she admits. "He was cute. He was Jewish. I needed to get away from your grandparents. So I married him."

She takes a bite of her roll.

"The timing was right," she adds.

So it was that simple: a business transaction devoid of the Talmudic guarantee that my parents were predestined for each other—bashert, they call it—and that after the ceremony and a little nookie in their hotel room, their souls would become one for all eternity.

In 1962, after a five-month courtship, they married, and my mother crossed the East River and moved into my father's bachelor apartment on East Seventy-Ninth Street and First Avenue, nudging the southern border of Yorkville where you could still hear pinched whispers complaining about das Juden at the strudel shops lining East Eighty-Sixth Street. My father's apartment was a twenty-first-floor Danish modern aerie decorated in high-gloss cherry reds and enameled blacks with an Arne Jacobsen sideboard leaning against one wall, real Hirshfeld sketches autographed to my father and framed in gleaming J. Pocker ebony and linen, a four-foot square Jackson Pollock knockoff hanging behind a massive black tufted silk sofa, and a silver Sputnik chandelier, which hovered like a satellite above the white Carrara marble foyer floor. My father's bachelor apartment was conveniently located just steps from an old-fashioned butcher shop run by a bespectacled Bavarian who knew that the diminutive Jewish advertising executive who strolled around town dressed like a WASP preferred Eisebein—smoked ham hock—to schnitzel, and had a standing weekly order for a three-rib pork roast stuffed with dried fruit. Before he met my mother, my father found respite and peace in his small kitchen, slow-cooking the forbidden meat for hours after returning home from dutifully visiting his Orthodox parents every Sunday, as though treyf itself could wash away the bitter memory of his violent childhood and the desperate yearning for his father's love, which my grandfather had reserved strictly for God.

When my mother moved in, she brought with her Gaga, who was attached to her daughter by an invisible tether as heavy as a dog's backyard chain; my mother slipped her a set of house keys that Gaga believed gave her carte blanche to take control of my parents' apartment and their life. She visited four times a week, arriving before eight in the morning, traveling by subway from her apartment in The Brussels. Gaga made herself at home in my parents' miniscule kitchen, scouring it from cabinet to cabinet, throwing out anything that was alien to her—my father's squeeze-tube pâté; pickled cocktail onions for his Gibsons; duck mousse in a can from Butterfield Market—and picked a fight with the Bavarian butcher from whom, after she called him the Nazi, there would be no more pork roasts forthcoming. Instead, she opened up an account at the local supermarket and anointed herself the domestic head of my parents' new household.

When my mother met my father and moved into his East Seventy-Ninth Street apartment, she thought she'd said goodbye to the provinces for good. The city was what she lived for, what she yearned for, and moving to an Upper East Side zip code was synonymous with the sort of success that announces its presence subtly: there would be no taxis back and forth to the dingy apartment she shared with her mother in Queens. Her life with her advertising executive husband would be one of museums and movies, music and fashion.

But two years later, with my infant self in tow, my mother returned to Forest Hills with her new husband, just in time for the

1964 World's Fair. They rented a two-bedroom apartment with a terrace in The Marseilles, directly across the courtyard from Gaga and overlooking The Champs-Élysées Promenade. Now a semisuburban family of three, they acquired Binky, a vicious miniature Schnauzer who peed on my father's pillow every morning, and an annual membership to The Fountainbleu swimming pool, which was attached to our building via a damp basement passageway adjacent to the communal laundry room and a locked bicycle closet. It was there, amidst a spiderweb of rusting Schwinn bicycle spokes, that the bored housewives of The Marseilles, with keys filched from our befuddled doormen, entertained their neighbors' older sons while their husbands were at work in the city, seven miles away.

APART FROM THE REQUISITE BAROQUE silver mezuzah that Gaga stuck to our front-door frame with Elmer's Glue and the twice-yearly father/daughter excursions to a shul in the far reaches of Coney Island where we watched my paternal grandfather, Henry, daven for hours, the extent of our devotion was limited to Gaga's roast chicken on Friday night; her potato latkes; and eight nights of orange electric menorah candles that flickered and buzzed during Hanukah.

Though we were not religious, we were surrounded by a sea of piety: follow The Champs-Élysées Promenade out to Austin Street and Sixty-Seventh Avenue and there, directly across the street from John's Candy Store, sat an ultra-Orthodox shul. Walk down Sixty-Seventh Avenue less than two blocks in the other direction, and you'd pass another one. Round the corner onto Queens Boulevard, past Ben's Best deli and the Ballet Academy, and there was the fanciful and modern Rego Park Jewish Center, adorned with magnificent stained-glass windows the colors of red and green maraschino cherries. Four long blocks the other way, past the Tung Shing House, stood Forest Hills Jewish Center, where Candy Feinblatt would be bat mitzvahed.

We belonged to none of them.

"You liff in a willage of shuls," Grandpa Henry admonished my father one day over bowls of cold borscht in his Coney Island kitchen, waving a bony, arthritic finger at him. "And you still can't find vone you like? Nothing's good enough for you, Mister Big Shot? Vhat are you? A Gentile? The baby needs to know she's Jewish."

He nodded over at me. I was the baby, even at ten.

My grandfather pulled a handkerchief out of his gray, pinstriped pocket and wiped smudges from his gold wire glasses. An émigré from a Ukrainian shtetl, Grandpa Henry arrived in the United States in 1905, the year the pogroms swept through the Pale of Settlement, killing thousands. As a twelve-year-old boy, he fled alone, running from the anti-Semitic terror of the time but also the quiet horror of his tiny dirt-floored household and the regular beatings doled out by a new stepfather who hated him. He said goodbye to his mother and brothers and ran west through Germany to France and then to England, arriving in New York after a stomach-churning transatlantic crossing. He set foot on the island of Manhattan lonely and starving; a peddler dragging a pushcart down Delancey Street took pity on him and gave him a banana. Cloying and unrecognizable, the fruit of the new world made him instantly sick. He retched over the railing of the Williamsburg Bridge, as if flinging off his past like his stepfather throwing bread into the Poltva River during Tashlikh, casting off his sins into the depths of the sea, as commanded by the Talmud.

"I vas alone, totally," he told me, when I was a child, "and I loved no vone but God."

"Tell me the story again," I would beg, gasping at the nerve he mustered to run away at twelve. And he would tell me again: the ass-whippings, the shame, the running, the crossing, the hunger, the pity, the banana.

Grandpa Henry grew into a devout Talmudic scholar who spent every moment he could in temple. Blessed with a deep, baritone singing voice, he became a cantor who sang with Jan Peerce and the Lower East Side klezmer star Naftule Brandwein. He took a job as the social page editor of the Yiddish newspapers *The Daily Forward* and then *The Day*, where he counted Zero Mostel and Molly Picon among his close friends. He was a benevolent and loving husband and father to his wife, daughter, and four granddaughters—I can see the eyes of my mother in your face, he would say, cradling my chin in his hand.

But to his son, my grandfather's dormant rage ran like a hot wire lashing generation to generation.

"Mister Big Shot. Who do you think you are, not to take the baby to shul?"

My father chuckled softly at the old man in a familiar, taunting way that balanced on the continuum between rage and reason. My reaction to the quiet, seething rage was panic: my breathing shallowed; I took sips of air like it was hot tea and looked at the two men, back and forth, over the table. There, in the silent moments before my father's explosion—in Forest Hills, it would be an ashtray thrown; a collar grabbed; his hips peeling away from the yellow vinyl seat of his chair so that he could reach me across the table—was a place as recognizable to me as my own breath.

I waited, staring at my bowl, holding the sides of my chair until my fingertips went numb.

My father's wooden chair squealed against the yellow scuffed linoleum as he shoved himself away from the table and stood; a blue glass bottle of seltzer wearing a silver mesh snood fell over and landed across a sleeve of saltines. My grandfather grabbed his son's wrist. My father's hand turned white.

"Sit down and eat, Schmeel," my grandfather said softly. "Tell me about vork."

My father's face was the same color as the borscht that had been placed in front of us. It was genetic memory: we both loathed the soup. Earthy, dusty, sweet, spicy, the magenta of my Crayola box, borscht tasted to me like dirt, like the vegetal scrapings from the bottomless schissels used to cook vast quantities of the pink gruel that would keep our ancestors alive long enough to be murdered by Cossacks and Nazis; it tasted of the past, and we choked on it. This is who you are, the soup said to us. This is who you will always, ever be.

Dos cyfele est nisht ken borscht, my father mumbled to my grandmother, who was puttering around behind us. The baby doesn't eat borscht.

Es vet esn maynem, she answered. She'll eat mine.

Mamenyu, ikh es im oykh nisht, my father said. Ma, I don't eat it either.

Vest im esn du oykh, she replied, padding around us in her house slippers. You'll eat it, too.

My father and I were two children at the same table, separated by a berth of forty years; to my grandparents, we were the same age.

My grandmother hung over me, her heavy bosom resting on my shoulder, and whacked a spoonful of sour cream into my soup plate, swirling it around and around until it resembled a dizzying rose and white kaleidoscope that made my stomach lurch and my head spin. She folded her arms and stared down at me while my grandfather watched and shook his head at me in disgust. I dipped the end of my spoon into the bowl and touched it to the end of my tongue. I swallowed and gasped; burning acid shot through my stomach and singed the back of my throat and I thought I'd vomit on the spot, right there, across my grandmother's petuniaflecked vinyl tablecloth. I got sick on the food of the old country, just as my grandfather had gotten sick on the food of the new.

"You'll eat it," Grandpa said to me without looking up, tapping his spoon against the side of his bowl. "Now, Schmeel, I vant to hear about vork."

THREE YEARS LATER, my grandfather came home from saying his morning prayers at shul, ate the same chopped chicken liver sandwich on rye that my grandmother fed him every day on the same blue and white Meissen plate, took his daily early afternoon nap, and never woke up. He was eighty-six.

Following Talmudic law and the tug of the primal on his shirtsleeve, my father said the Mourner's Kaddish—the obligatory prayer for the dead—every morning for a year, the time period that the deceased is considered to be under the threat of divine judgment. After my mother served us soft-boiled eggs with thin slices of diet white bread, my father and I walked Binky through the dank basement, past the communal laundry room, and up towards The Champs-

Élysées Promenade to meet my school bus. My father's lips moved silently and his eyes filled with tears as he mumbled the five-thousand-year-old Aramaic prayer, turning his back to me.

I dragged along behind him in my nylon olive green snorkel parka and brown corduroy bell-bottoms, my canvas knapsack hanging heavy and low on the small of my back. I hummed something from television.

He spun around and jammed his index finger against his mouth.

Y' hei sh' lama raba min sh'maya
V'chayim aleinu v'al kol Yisrael
V'imru: Amen.

May there be abundant peace from heaven, and life
For us and all Israel,
To which we say Amen.

I hummed.

He turned, his still lips curling in furious, compulsory devotion, and pounded his fist on the locked bicycle room door.

"Stop noodging!" he raged. "Can't you see what I'm doing?" We emerged from the basement out into the bright morning light that made me squint. I climbed up the school bus stairs and sat down next to Candy; I watched my father through the bus window as we pulled away. He stood with the dog, talked to Eugene, and lit his day's second cigarette.

For a year, my father prayed where no one but I could see him; it was our secret. He chanted silently in the dark of the clammy cellar, as we passed the entrance to the garage beneath The Marseilles; prayer felt dangerous and shameful, and something to be hidden from the world around us. The sanctity that my father was drawn to tortured him; as we descended into the bowels of our building, he choked on hot tears as he chanted like the dutiful son he was, ignoring the portion of the law that also commands that the Mourner's Kaddish be said in a synagogue, provided there is one in walking distance.

In our case, there were four.

4

Mad Men

M Y FATHER WAS a Fifth Avenue mad man ad man of the teak cre-
denza–Modern Jazz Quartet variety, who was obsessed with
Clint Eastwood, Chopin, and British equestriana to the degree that
by the time I was nine, he had taught me to name every part of an
English bridle, hauling me out at parties to show our inebriated
neighbors what his daughter, who had never been near or on a horse,
knew. My friends wore bell-bottoms and traded Mets baseball cards
and memorized the names of *The Partridge Family*: Shirley, Keith,
Laurie, Danny, Chris, Tracy, Mr. Kincaid. I proudly explained the
difference between a seven-gaited horse and a five-gaited gelding
and was frequently dressed in the smaller version of the matching
mother-daughter houndstooth tweed hacking jacket and jodhpur
outfits my father bought for us at H. Kauffman and Sons, the riding
store on East Twenty-Fourth Street in Manhattan.

When summer became autumn, my mother and I donned our
riding clothes for everyday activities like going to the mall or to Alex-
ander's, our local department store that carried everything from no-

tions to monkeys. Off we'd go, my size two mother in her blue-lensed Jean Shrimpton aviators and her sleek blond hair swept back in a tiny ponytail held in place with a black velvet bow, and me in my miniature Prince of Wales tweed hacking jacket, riding pants, and hunting boots; our neighbor's heads turned as we'd march out onto the Champs-Élysées Promenade and up to Austin Street, past John's Candy Store and the neighboring pizza shop, which shared a wall with Tony's Shoe Repair. Every pizza pie stank from the pungent blend of shoe polish and warm leather, and every pair of my mother's resoled riding boots reeked from garlic and pork sausage.

"Everyone's staring at us," I'd wail, when our neighbors looked at us and pointed. I hung on to my mother's manicured hand like a chimp.

"Don't be silly," she'd say. "It's only because they're jealous.

Now hold your head up. Let's go."

My mother taught me to stride like a model, to keep my shoulders forward and still, and sashay smoothly from my nonexistent hips, one foot behind the other. We strolled through Forest Hills as though we were on a catwalk, stopping to talk to whomever we ran into. There was Tess, who owned the dry cleaning shop down the street and expunged the secrets of every local marriage. Sallow and gaunt with a missing front tooth and a crackling voice like the Wicked Witch of the West, she reeked of the gin that she carried in a silver flask in her gray smock pocket, which clanged against the counter when she leaned forward to give us my father's freshly laundered suits. We frequently ran into Marion Feinblatt and Candy exiting the Ballet Academy on Queens Boulevard, where Candy was studying to become the next Gelsey Kirkland. Laura Steinman would stop us to chat, offering my mother a Virginia Slims; they'd stand there, puffing away, sizing each other up like two wrestlers in a ring, neither of them noticing that nine-year-old Stuey was trying to pin me up against a parked car so that he could jam his sweaty little hand down my English riding pants. Raven-haired Judith Garbfeld, whose cheekbones were set as high on her head as her brown eyes, and who had just moved in next door to us with her Orthodox husband (or was it her boyfriend? We never knew for sure), Moishe, and their ten-year-old daughter, Shaina, never smiled and kept her terse chit-chat to a minimum. When Judith saw us in our riding habits, she stared us, head to toe, up and down, and sighed.

"I just love your costumes," she said, grinning. "Keep walking," my mother whispered to me.

Judith was skeptical, a smug eye-roller, like the life she found herself living in was an error. The neighbors whispered: Are they married? Is Shaina his? If not, who does she belong to? Jews don't live together. It was the building mystery, and the subject of dinner party conjecture among the neighbors, who gossiped as though we were still living in a small shtetl. Shaina, bucktoothed and flat-chested, never smiled, like her mother; she went to a yeshiva, kept to herself, and screamed at her mother in Hebrew, which I could hear through the wall that separated our bedrooms.

"Don't get too friendly with her," Gaga said, shaking a finger at me.

My father and I were in the elevator one morning when Moishe stepped on. When the door closed and we were alone with him, he asked my father, Were you in the camps?

It was the bind that connected Jew to Jew, survivor to survivor in the sixties and seventies; I heard old women ask it in my grandfather's shul near Coney Island. Were you in the camps? they whispered to each other. Their faces dropped, palsied, when the answer was yes; they pushed up a sleeve to reveal a faded green number tattooed on their forearm. I looked away; I had been told not to stare.

My father shook his head no and straightened his tie.

"Us neither," Moishe sighed, pushing back his black fedora a little. "But the Nazis came when Judith was five. Her parents left her with the local Catholics, walked into the field behind their farm, and shot themselves. Judith ran away and hid in the forests with the Partisans. She killed her first Nazi at seven. We met in Israel."

The elevator rattled against the brick shaft; sweat trickled through my father's graying sideburns.

"Zei gezunt," Moishe said when the door opened. "Have a good day at school, little girl," he added, gazing down at me.

My father and I walked out of the elevator in silence; we stepped out of the lobby into the morning sun and when the school bus pulled up in front of the luncheonette the way it did every day, he reached down and hugged me tightly, as though someone had just died.

MY FATHER'S LOVE FOR HORSES came from a childhood spent glued to "The Lone Ranger" radio broadcasts, dreaming of the freedom that hoofbeats evoked for a city-bound boy living in a two-bedroom apartment stinking of schmaltz. It might have also been the promise of control: a slight, thin Jewish boy on the back of a massive beast, manipulating it, directing it, riding with the wind at his back like Audie Murphy. He loved them all: old horses, young ones, tall ones, short ones, but especially the rickety, even-tempered ones he would ride on lazy ambles through the hills surrounding the singles' dude ranch he visited every weekend towards the end of the 1950s, before he married my mother. Like many other New York City ad men of the time, he left Manhattan at the end of the workweek, but instead of pointing his rental car towards the borscht belt, he headed instead for a non-Jewish part of Orange County, sixty miles from the city. Every Friday night, from the early spring into midwinter when it became too cold to ride, my father drove an hour north, arriving for predinner gin Gibsons at the ranch's immense, timber-framed, German Tudor-style main house. There, in the cavernous living room, he met single ladies who also spent their country weekends riding ancient horses with barely a pulse, acquired by the ranch for equestrian neophytes who didn't know a saddle from an edsel. Dressed in tweed jackets, dusty whipcord jodhpurs, and knee-high hunting boots, my father and his harem dined on what was billed by the ranch as the Finest European Country Cuisine—sauerbraten and spaetzle and escargot and chateaubriand—and spent the weekends living the lives of landed gentry before going home to their tiny apartments in Manhattan, Brooklyn, and Queens to get ready for the workweek ahead of them.

My father ceased being a dude when the ranch fell into disrepair and eventually shut down, and his carefree days riding the imaginary range were relegated to memory. His boots, the loosethighed Knickerbocker jodhpurs that made him look like a Canadian Mountie, and his beloved shearling ranch coat were all he had left of his horsey bachelor life when he married my mother. She got rid of the coat when I was five, convinced that it was making her bedroom smell like a barnyard.

"Pee-EWW," she cried, pulling open her closet door.

My mother pinched her nose and twisted her face in dramatic disgust while Binky and I watched from the bed. Her blond hair had just been trimmed and sprayed into a George, and tiny bits of it still clung to her tight black turtleneck and denim hiphuggers. She pushed up her sleeves and the gold charm bracelet that hung off her arm, reached in, shoved my father's suits, pants, and sport jackets to one side, pulled out the coat, and held it up for inspection. It was the color of dirty caramel, and a darkened, ancient stain adorned the right patch pocket from the time when my father's favorite gelding had dipped his head and horked up a thick wad of spit and hay and snot while my father was saddling him ten years earlier.

"What do we think about this?" my mother asks me, that afternoon. She shows me the coat, front and back, back and front.

"Daddy's horse coat—" I say, proudly identifying it.

"Let's buy him a new one," my mother says brightly. "We'll pick it out together."

I clutch my knees to my chest and begin to rock; we never shop for my father together.

She folds the coat over her arm and walks out of the bedroom, out our front door, and down the hallway to the incinerator. I follow—my heart races; I know how much my father loves it—and watch as she props the heavy metal door open with one foot, and stuffs the odorous garment down the chute.

My father arrives home from work that night, kicks off his shoes, opens his closet, hangs up his suit jacket, and inhales deeply. The pungent essence of horse sweat, sweet to him as Proust's madeleine, is gone.

Instead, Lysol.

I watch from my parents' bed, their bedroom television set blaring *Laugh-In*, as he tears through the contents of his closet, frantically pushing each hanger aside: there's the blue striped suit, the brown striped suit, the blue seersucker suit, the navy blazer, the camel's hair blazer, the banker's gray pants, the terrycloth robe, the riding jodhpurs, the Glen plaid hacking jacket, the powder blue leisure suit with the white buttons accidentally melted by Tess during an overzealous dry cleaning. He shoves everything back and starts all over again, like a shopper searching a rack for the right size. His ears are so red, they're almost blue. I can hear my mother in the kitchen, opening the refrigerator door; I hear her pull the cork on a bottle of wine. From where I sit, I can see my father's dingy white Jack Purcells, his brown loafers, his wingtips, his tan suede bucks, his riding boots, his leather opera slippers lined up on the closet floor. A colorful cardboard box containing his electric race car set topples over from where it is leaning against the inside closet wall; the lid separates from the bottom and long sections of black plastic track fall out and into the entryway to the bedroom. He grabs them and heaves all but one back into the closet; that one he smashes against the wall, until it explodes into shards of extruded black plastic that fly everywhere.

"Where is it?" he yells. My mother is watching from the narrow hallway between their bedroom and mine, smoking a cigarette and sipping her wine from a blue glass goblet.

"Not in front of her," she says, calmly, nodding over to me on the bed.

"Where IS it?"

"It stank like a stable. I'll get you a new one." She draws a puff and the tip of her cigarette grows into a long, smoldering ash the length of a pencil eraser. I'm fixated on it; if it drops, I'm certain that it will set the wall-to-wall carpet on fire like on the television shows I watch, and we will burn and we will perish and the building will be a hollowed-out shell of brick, the blackened holes where windows used to be now empty and gaping like toothless sockets.

My father slams the closet door, which jolts me out of my pyrophobic panic. He storms into the foyer, pulls out an ancient, hard-sided brown tweed Pullman suitcase, drags it past my mother and her cigarette back into the bedroom, and flings it open onto their bed right next to me; its leather handle grazes my leg. He empties a drawer's worth of clothes into it, slams it shut, and stomps out into the hallway, grabs his car keys from the candy dish on the entryway table, and pulls the front door closed behind him so hard that the doorbell rings and the dog barks.

It happens in thick, slow motion; I watch it like a movie, through a scrim, from a distance.

The mother, heavily made up like a movie starlet, is talking to the small child lying on her parents' bed. The mother's mouth moves slowly. The child's lips are parted; she's barely breathing. She's sweating a little; she's shivering. Her color has gone sallow. She vomits all over her flannel pajamas, the powder blue ones with the tiny apples; there is Hawaiian Punch everywhere.

"Don't worry, honey," the mother says to the child, taking her by the hand into the bathroom where she sits her on the toilet and tenderly strips off her soaked and wretched pajamas. She washes her daughter's face with a cool washcloth that's lost its nap; it feels like cold sandpaper on the child's face. "He'll be back," she says, while the child sits stunned, exhausted.

"He'll be back," the child whispers to herself.

The child has heard the parent-had-to-leave fairy tale over and over again; she's heard it over dinner and she's heard it in the car and she's heard it while being tucked in, sometimes instead of Dr. Seuss. Her father's mother left the family when her father was three years old, but ultimately, she loved them and couldn't stay away; she came back to them eventually, and they lived happily ever after. He has spoon-fed this tale of abandonment to the child like pabulum—there's no wolf or witch or getting lost in a forest in his bedtime story; desertion itself is the villain, abandonment the scoundrel, hovering like a cloud, always threatening—from the time she understands words and can comprehend their meaning, and the meaning behind their meaning. He tells the story not as a warning, but as a lesson, a parable, a statement of fact: sometimes, parents leave.

"And then," he would say to the child, "she left."

And then, she left. She left.

"But then," he says, beaming, "she came back. And they lived happily ever after."

He kisses her on the forehead and the child hugs his neck and nuzzles his rough cheek and he settles her down deep between the white sheets dotted with faded pink roses and fuchsia.

She came back.

The child brightens and sleeps soundly.

The night he leaves, the screen fades as I sit on the toilet while my mother washes my face; I have no memory of being put in bed, but I wake up the next morning in that short sliver of time where everything feels normal until it doesn't, and routine is the tenuous plank that connects sleep to waking. I lower the metal guardrail on the side of my bed that keeps me from rolling out onto the dark green carpet, and, like I do every morning, I run into my parents' bedroom and fling myself on their bed; for a few minutes, until I see his side still tightly made, his pillow cold and untouched—my mother is already up and in the bathroom, putting on her makeup— I've forgotten that he's gone. My mother and I are alone together in the apartment; she steps out of the bathroom and asks if I like her new eyeshadow color; she's trying powder blue for a change.

I NEVER KNEW WHERE HE went or whether he intended to leave us for good. But two days later, my father came back, as my mother assured me he would. When he returned, my mother threw on her coat and went downstairs to the kosher butcher on Austin Street and bought nine baby lamb chops for what I was sure would be a celebratory meal; she deposited them in a foil tray, drizzled them with vegetable oil, and shoved them under the broiler until they ignited like dry kindling and angry blue flames licked up and out of the bottom of the stove, blackening our white Chambers oven door. I shrieked and ran into my bedroom with the dog while my mother languidly beat at them with a greasy kitchen towel.

"Dinner!" she yelled, and my father and I came back to the kitchen and sat at the table. The three of us ate in silence, the little Zenith television at the end of the kitchen table blaring news about Saigon; we scraped thick black layers of immolated fat off our chops, picked them up, and gnawed them down to the bone, the bitter taste of food cooked in anger filling our mouths. It was as though nothing had happened; as long as she was feeding her husband dinner, there was hope, even if it was incinerated.

On the Saturday morning after his return, my father appeared in my bedroom doorway dressed like he was going fox hunting—jodhpurs, boots, gray-green tweed blazer—instead of for a walk out onto The Champs-Élysées Promenade with the dog. He returned an hour later carrying a heavy paper bag; while I watched from a kitchen stool, he set one of my mother's scuffed Teflon pans on the stove and opened a small rectangular metal can with a key that came attached to its bottom. Using a butter knife, he pried the gelatinous pink brick out of the can; it slid out with a sickening splat onto a gold-banded white plate from my mother's wedding china. My father sliced it into thick rafts and in the dry skillet fried the slices in their own fat until great clouds of smoky pork essence rose around us like a mushroom cloud, making my eyes tear and the dog drool.

My father carefully flipped the spluttering, crispy planks, and broke six eggs into the pan, cooking them until the whites were firm and the yolks just set. He portioned the meat and the eggs out onto three plates and set them down alongside each other. We sat down to eat at our counter, side by side in silence; he reached over me to slice my breakfast into small squares. When he was done, he cut his up the same way.

The Spam was tender and unctuous and encased in a crackling jacket of golden, fried pork fat. It was salty and bitter and rich; it tasted of spite and fury and betrayal, and clandestine flavors that I had never tasted before.

We sat together in silence and ate. "Good?" he said.

I nodded.

My father read the *Times* and lifted fork to mouth, fork to mouth, not looking up when my mother walked into the kitchen, dressed for the day in her favorite brown wool blazer and tan suede jeans, a blue and gold silk Hermès horse-bit scarf tied around her neck. Her plate sat on the counter next to mine; her breakfast was cold. She picked up the empty can, squinted at it, and threw it into the garbage.

"We're Jews," she said, scraping the Spam and eggs directly into the trash and dumping her plate into the sink. She turned on the water and blasted away the sheen of pork fat and sticky yolk.

"We don't leave our children. And we don't eat dog food."

5

The Neighbors

THERE WERE THE SYNAGOGUES and the kosher butchers, the Tung Shing House and the Oasis, and the bar mitzvahs that took place every Saturday in 1974. But Forest Hills—before Son of Sam and after Kitty Genovese, who was murdered in 1964 a few blocks from The Marseilles while her neighbors famously pulled closed their shutters against her screams—was a mixed community of residents with one foot planted squarely in the past and the other shuffling clumsily into the future like a sweatypalmed boy learning the fox-trot. For many, the town was a midway point, a way station to breathe and refuel, a not-quite-verdant pit stop stuck between the grimness of first generation Brooklyn and the Bronx, and the promise of the Long Island border towns, which my father called The Golden Ghetto, and where, almost without exception, we all dreamed of living.

When I was a young child and just learning how to read, Gaga and my parents filled my bedroom with books; there were colorful storybooks and alphabet books, books of light verse and a set of illustrated presidential biographies that arrived once a month through a Time Life children's subscription that my father had ordered for me. There was a spine-broken, taped-together hardcover copy of D'Aulaires' *Book of Greek Myths*, which had been handed down to me by Aunt Sylvia from her youngest daughter, Sarah, and which I slept clutching under my covers the way some children do a stuffed toy, so enamored was I of my teenage cousin that her castoffs felt to me like love itself. My parents and Gaga read to me constantly: Gaga preferred poetry, and I knew the first lines of The Song of Hiawatha before I was five; my mother liked the singsong simplicity of Dr. Seuss. When Gaga and my mother weren't looking, my father devised his own way of teaching me how to read that was more practical and produced immediate results: he handed me a heavy catalog of toys from FAO Schwarz. My eyes bugged: there were pictures of stuffed animals, sulkies meant to be pulled by actual small ponies, gorgeous wooden blocks in brilliant colors. He showed me how to match the letter next to the toy to its description: a matched up to a watery-eyed German teddy bear, its arms open in beckoning love, from a company called Steiff; b connected to a life-size, Tudor-style dollhouse big enough for a small child to stand up in. Surrounded by children's books piled in every corner of my bedroom, I learned how to read by analyzing advertising copy for things I longed for, but would never actually own. I lived in a state of constant want—so desirous of this stuff I was certain I'd die without it—but I was reading chapter books by the time I was six. It was want, my father believed, that would push me and motivate me, and drive me to success; chronic disappointment was something he didn't count on, although he knew it like the color of his own eyes.

Less than ten miles from the eraser-pink brick building we lived in in the shadow of the Queens Boulevard traffic snarl were the pristine country clubs, golf courses, and yacht clubs of my father's dreams. There were closets bursting with St. John suits and headlight-sized diamonds worn beneath expertly lacquered fingernails; there were skiing vacations to Sun Valley and customized, boat-sized Mercedes sedans, the ultimate status symbol of the time, with their hood ornaments sliced off to hide the vehicles' German provenance a mere thirty years after the war.

Every Sunday, after our dutiful, staccato visits to Coney Island to see my father's parents, we pointed our massive Buick towards King's Point—Jay Gatsby's West Egg—where his advertising agency's real estate clients had been dotting the area with hastily built contemporary split-levels and ranch houses since the end of the 1940s. We drove from model home to model home—ten of them in a day, ostensibly part of my father's job, but not much different for him than my FAO Schwarz catalog—and for years, I believed that we were forever on the verge of moving. I envisioned a yard, a carport like the Bradys had, and a place to throw around a football with Gaga.

"Are we buying this one?" I'd say, dropping my mother's hand and racing through fake avocado green model kitchens filled with fake avocado green model appliances and basement dens carpeted with fake avocado green broadloom, and bathrooms adorned with fake harvest gold toilets that I, more than once, peed in.

"We'll see," my father would answer, opening and closing closet doors like an inspector.

"I'm never living on Long Island," my mother insisted every time, her arms folded across her chest. "I'm a city girl."

"But the schools are so good out here," he'd say.

"They're fine where we are, too—" she'd say.

"We could have a yard—"

"You're gonna mow? We don't need a yard."

"But look at the kitchen—it's enormous."

"I hate to cook."

"You could have new neighbors—"

"I like our old neighbors."

Weekend after weekend, year after year, we made the long drive out to Long Island to see the houses my father advertised, until they began to blur like smeared ink into one wood-paneled, game-roomed beacon of hope and promise of success that my father wanted so badly he could taste it.

THERE WERE FEW SECRETS IN The Marseilles and The Brussels; the walls were too thin, the hundreds of apartments jammed together like sardines so that every fight, every cry of anger or ecstasy could be heard, every rasher of bacon smelled as though neighbors were all living under the same roof, which they were. There were the Pugaches—Burt and Linda—she of the darkened glasses, famously blinded for life when the enraged Burt, who was having an affair with her that she ended, hired three men to throw lye in her face in a jealous fit. He went to jail for fourteen years before marrying her and settling down in The Brussels, just upstairs from my grandmother. There was gossiping Laura Steinman, who lacquered her skin to the color of a football with the sunless tanner QT and whose face, my father once remarked over dinner, resembled a rotting apple core; her husband, Richard, gave off great, billowing clouds of Jovan Musk and could be seen walking around The Champs-Élysées Promenade in a stained, cream-colored trench coat, whatever the weather. There were the Garbfelds, who were possibly married and possibly not, and their daughter, Shaina, who might have been Moishe's child or might have not. Whenever we saw her, Judith spent as much time eying my mother's unique outfits as my mother did hers; Judith wore tight polyester hip-huggers in bright colors and puffed-sleeved blazers over too-short blouses that revealed a ribbon of putty-colored flesh. Waiting for the elevator together, they gaped at each other like gladiators: Judith stared at my mother's riding outfits. My mother gawked at the roll of creamy fat that bulged between the top of Judith's pants and the bottom of her shirt. The tension between them cleaved to the air like humidity.

The enmity between the Steinmans, the Garbfelds, and my parents was mutual; they were never invited to us, nor we to them. Instead, my mother and father did their cocktail partying to Trini Lopez and Peggy Lee, and their coffee and Entenmann's after a movie with a small coterie of other couples, all of them mixed-faith, who lived in the buildings.

My mother's best friend, Inga Hoffmann, was an earthy, warm-hearted redhead who loved to laugh, and who had grown up in a devout Lutheran home in Nazi-occupied Copenhagen. Inga was married to George Hoffmann, a bug-eyed, potbellied itinerant magi-

cian whose most notable physical characteristic was that his feet
drastically turned outward, making it impossible to know which direction he was heading in when he walked. George performed regularly at my birthday parties, turning everything—our dog's Milk-Bones,
a red silk hankie, a small budgie—into a burst of yellow flame that
exploded from the depths of a threadbare Goodwill top hat, and sent
me hurtling to the floor where I cowered in terror. He employed his
children, Eddie and Tor, in his magic tricks: he ran a narrow, almost
invisible wire from a small magic button in his trouser pocket down
the leg of his triple-weave trousers and up into the pants' leg and
shirtsleeves of his two boys, and down into a tiny battery that they
held in their closed hands. While the boys waited in silence for their
cue, George casually zapped his sons with shocks when he asked
them in front of a rapt audience of six-year-olds to Go on, guess how
many scarves Daddy is going to pull out of his magic top hat, and
they'd wince accordingly: once, twice, three times, four, or five.

"Five scarves, Daddy," towheaded Eddie Hoffmann would miraculously guess, smiling through his stubby, clenched baby teeth,
his Sta-Prest white shirt and tiny black clip-on tie damp with sweat.

Inga and the boys left George in New York for two months every
summer and went to Denmark, where her mother still lived.

When she returned home with Eddie and Tor at the end of August, my mother and I would spend our late afternoons at the Hoffmann apartment in The Brussels, which with every passing summer
became increasingly festooned with all manner of imported Danish
foods, paintings of rock-jawed Scandinavian sea captains, yellow
Dansk Kobenstyle cookware, small rubber trolls, and miniature statues of helmeted Vikings that Inga carried back to New York with her.
Her sliver of a galley kitchen had been packed with processed junk
foods before she left for Denmark every summer: there were bags of
Funions, boxes of PopTarts, jars of Tang, cans of spray cheese, sour
Slim Jims smelling of rancid pork fat. But when she came home
from Copenhagen, she made a clean sweep of her cupboards, replacing everything with the Scandinavian foods that she loved. Every
day after picking Eddie and me up from the school bus, my mother

and Inga planted themselves for hours at Inga's tiny table opposite her stove. While Eddie and I played Eric the Red or Rape and Plunder in the bedroom that he shared with Tor, Inga poured my mother cold goblets of Soave Bolla and fed her warm, sugar-dusted lefse, whisper-thin slices of boiled Danish ham, Jarlsberg, and wedges of Gjetost Ski Queen, a chocolate brown goat cheese made from caramelized goats' milk and solidified into a block of cloyingly sweet nuttiness. Tipsy and counting the slender hours of freedom before their husbands returned from work in the city, Inga served my mother on heavy brown earthenware plates; cigarette in one hand and wineglass in the other, my mother nibbled what was put in front of her— the warm bread, the cheese, the cool salty boiled meat as forbidden as the Spam my father had cooked the day after he returned to us.

Tor, who was four years older than Eddie and me, had better things to do than play Eric the Red: he spent his afternoons tossing rocks off a Grand Central Parkway overpass onto the windshields of oncoming cars, pulling the legs off spiders while they sizzled under a magnifying glass in the sun, and setting fires in empty lots around our neighborhood. One Sunday when I was twelve and Tor was sixteen—before his incarceration, his heroin addiction, his eventual suicide—and Eddie had gone out to ride his new Apollo 8 bicycle, Tor grabbed my wrist hard like a handcuff, pulled me into his bedroom, forced me down onto his tartan blanket, and attempted to relieve me of my virginity while my mother did her Peggy Lee imitation for Inga, George, and my father, just steps away in the Hoffmann living room. Tor was tall and narrow, always dressed in the same sky-blue, slightly dirty Levi bell-bottoms and tight plaid button-down shirt, a hormonal mass of ropy sinew and weeping acne, a fresh brown stubble sprouting like new grass along his pimpled jawline.

It'll . . . make you . . . Danish, Tor growled in my ear, furiously humping me like a bronco rider on his narrow single bed beneath his shelf of tiny rubber Vikings, his face crimson, his blond hair glued with sweat to the sides of his head.

Get off, I said, trying to push him away, and he did.

Fuuuck, he groaned. Fuck—fuck. Christ. Fuck. And then, nothing.

I pushed and shoved him off me and made a grab for the doorknob and we rolled out of his bedroom, tumbling like weeds into the hallway, my puffed-sleeve bandana shirt half unbuttoned, a dark indigo splotch blossoming on the front of his faded Levi's.

"Enough, both of you—be quiet—she's singing," George said from the couch, pointing over to my mother, who stood in front of his maple spinet piano and snapped her fingers, her arm straight in front of her, palm down. She knit her brow in a tight furrow above her heavily lined, unblinking brown eyes just like Peggy and whispered, Fever all through the day. I stood frozen in place and watched her performance with my father, Inga, and George, while Tor popped open a can of Fresca in the kitchen. My heart banged against the inside of my chest as she sang to us while a heavy brown platter of glistening ham and aging Gjetost sat on the modern teak end table, sweating in the heat of the apartment.

BUCK BERKOWITZ, my father's best friend, lived a few flights below us with his perpetually scowling Catholic wife, Velma, who wore her chocolate brown 1950s updo Aqua Netted to a standstill. Possessed of a screeching voice like nails on a chalkboard, tortoiseshell cat-eye glasses, and pearl gray twin sets, their arms stuffed to the elbows with used Kleenex, Velma kept her husband at an arm's length; when he went to hug her, she pushed him away. When he went to kiss her, she gave him a cheek. A man with the muscular shoulders of an all-American Ivy League tackle, Buck was an eight-by-ten glossy, my mother used to say, with hair so black it was almost blue, and a Brylcreemed spit curl that sat glued to the middle of his forehead, like a comma. Obsessed with Chihuahuas and his perfectly square white Chiclet teeth, which he would have cleaned monthly at the dentist whose office was on the ground floor of The Brussels, Buck was a math teacher at a local Catholic boys' high school and utterly devoted to children and their well-being.

As much as Buck loved children was exactly how much Velma loathed them; their daughter, Darleen, born with spina bifida, seemed to exhaust Velma with every pull and drag of her child's heavy wheelchair, her every need to be tended, morning and night. Over a pizza and Tang dinner one night at their powder blue apartment when I was ten, I caught Velma glaring at me across their mahogany dining room table after Buck and my parents had stepped outside onto the terrace to have a cigarette.

"What?" I whispered to her across the pile of oil-stained pizza boxes, while Darleen, sitting next to me on a square couch pillow, played with her food. *The Glen Campbell Goodtime Hour* blared from the abandoned television in the living room.

"Nothing, Elissa," Velma sighed. She shook her head, pushed herself away from the table, stood up, flattened out her apron, and slunk into the bedroom, alone; I heard the click of the button in the doorknob.

VELMA HAD MOVED TO NEW YORK from eastern Kansas in 1954 to launch an acting career that never took off; instead, she was relegated to odd jobs as a hand double in short television commercials for second-tier products, like Rinso Soap, the camera stopping just north of her slender wrists. Ten years later, she met Buck at a party—recently divorced and handsome beyond her wildest dreams—married him, gave birth to Darleen, and spent most of her time dressed in a flowered cotton apron in their kitchen in The Marseilles, turning out breakfast, lunch, and dinner for her new family: her freezer was stockpiled with Swanson frozen dinners—honey-fried chicken, the complete turkey dinner, Salisbury steak, Welsh rarebit—for every occasion. The only time she actually cooked anything from scratch was at Christmas, when she produced a ham for me, my parents, Buck and Darleen, and the Hoffmanns, as a show, she announced, of Christian goodwill. The size of a beach ball, it was served studded with cloves and canned pineapple rings held in place with red- and green-dyed toothpicks that bled into the meat while it sat roasting for hours in their Caloric oven. When it was ready, Velma dragged it out and onto a mottled-glass cutting board while my parents, Inga, George, Tor, Eddie, Darleen, and I played with the three Berkowitz Chihuahuas and helped Buck unpack cardboard shoeboxes filled with plastic Victorian carolers in top hats and bonnets, their tiny red mouths shaped into perfect Os.

"Buck!" Velma would bleat from the kitchen. "Have them set up the carolers on the mantelpiece!"

Buck lifted up the white plastic fireplace that had sat propped against the living room wall since Thanksgiving, and hung it off two small metal picture hooks. One by one, Eddie and Tor and I took turns positioning the tiny carolers on the fake mantelpiece. Switched on, the fireplace played an endless loop of Mantovani Christmas music while a small fan blew three orange velvet ribbons against a hard plastic backdrop onto which was painted a flaming Yule log. Darleen, sitting in her wheelchair and dressed like a much younger child in a red velvet jumper flecked with tiny green reindeer, her legs encased in white Danskin leotards, howled with glee and applauded. Buck scooped her out of her chair and bounced her and her rubbery toy Rudolph over to the fireplace, where she stood the reindeer up in the middle of the arrangement and cooed.

"Just like Tiny Tim!" Tor shouted.

"Don't be an asshole," my father mumbled, grabbing Tor's collar and pulling him away from the fireplace while George and Inga huddled together on the terrace, away from the festivities, their backs to their children, watching the Christmas lights flicker over The Champs-Élysées Promenade.

Once the ham was eaten and small bowls of vanilla ice cream topped with maraschino cherries were sucked down, Buck, Darleen, my father, and I bundled ourselves up and took the dogs out for a nighttime walk. While my father held the leashes of all four dogs, Buck bent down at my feet and zipped up my Mighty Mac, gently tousling my hair when he reached my chin; I loved him for his tenderness, but stopped myself from telling him so.

"It's f-r-e-e-z-i-n-g—aren't you cold, honey?" He fakeshivered, and helped me into my mittens. I wanted to fling my arms around his neck, rest my head on his shoulder and never let go.

Buck picked up the Chihuahuas and set them down on a thread-bare blue towel draped across Darleen's lap, and I pushed her along in her wheelchair, her motionless legs pointed straight out in front of her. My father and Buck followed slowly behind us as I struggled to maneuver my friend's leaden weight into the promenade and up to Austin Street. I wheeled her past John's Candy Store and Tess's Dry Cleaning towards the Associated grocery at the end of the block. We stopped, alone, under the glare of a streetlight, as though it were any other ordinary winter evening, and I pulled the brake lever on Dar-leen's wheelchair; Austin Street was like a barren Hollywood back lot: there was not a single holiday display coloring the cold gray sky. The dogs perched on her lap, Darleen looked forward with an unsure grin, wide-eyed and unblinking, as if to the future and towards some-thing only she could see. Our fathers came up behind us, talking about Long Island—the South Shore versus the North, where the better school districts were—and who would be able to move their family out to the suburbs first to get away from the griminess and danger of the city.

"We can go any time," I heard Buck say to my father, who stopped to light two cigarettes, one for each of them, in his hand cupped against the cold.

I waited for them to catch up to us, their only children and their dogs, and I reached forward to gently touch the back of Darleen's head with a gloved hand; even through the wool, her dark brown hair felt delicate and silky, like an infants'. She was fragile and suddenly, I knew, somehow, that she would die. My throat clutched the way it did when I was about to weep, and something warm climbed into my chest towards my heart, and engulfed it.

6

Christmas

E VERY NIGHT, there is another celebrity Christmas special to watch
on television: The Osmond Brothers, singing carols from Temple
Square in Salt Lake City, enormous flakes of snow settling down on
their thick, gorgeous Mormon eyelashes. John Denver, wearing a
metallic silver, yoke-front Western-style shirt performs from inside a
heated glass geodesic dome atop a mountain in Aspen, while Annie
Denver and a group of their hippie friends watch contemplatively
through matching round granny glasses. There's *The Andy Williams
Christmas Show* and *The Partridge Family*, *The Brady Bunch*, the
Carpenters, Bob Hope, and Dean Martin, who sings Ave Maria.
There's Perry Como, who my mother swoons over, and when Bing
Crosby sings "The Little Drummer Boy" with David Bowie, I yell for
Gaga, who is frying potato latkes in our kitchen.

I am not allowed to have a Christmas tree—my father believes
that it's symbolic of everything Christian and pagan, and it would
certainly kill his Orthodox father if he ever found out about it—even
though my mother had one as a child. She grew up in Williamsburg

among a sea of Catholic neighbors, like Grandpa Phil's best friend, Sister Redempta, who ran a parochial school for orphaned boys.

"It was really just a holiday bush," my mother tells me and my father while we drive home from a shopping trip to Macy's, where he lets me pick out Hanukah gifts for Tor and Eddie and Darleen. On our way out of the store, my parents plunk me down on the lap of the store Santa and snap a picture. In it, I am smiling and looking away coyly while Santa asks me what I want for Christmas and I say, A Christmas tree and my father grabs my hand and yanks me out of the store and out to the car.

Gaga comes running down the hallway, nearly tripping over the dog, and her eyes grow misty when she sees the actor and the rocker—Bing in a blue golf sweater, Bowie in a tight shirt, a massive gold cross dangling around his neck as though he himself might be crucified. They're standing on a set decorated like an empty parish house attached to a very old church, with a piano and a Gothic window behind the two singers.

"My favorite song," Gaga says wistfully, standing over me in my bedroom with a Teflon spatula in one hand and an oily kitchen towel in the other. We watch the little Sony Trinitron television that my parents have given me for Hanukah; she begins to croon in a low, guttural mezzo-soprano with one of the most bizarre duets ever assembled for modern television, between a 1940s movie star with a strong religious, right-wing streak and a space oddity who sometimes goes by the name of Ziggy Stardust and apparently likes boys. And sometimes, girls.

Come they told me, pa rum pum pum pum.

Gaga loves this song; she's loved it since she first heard it on the radio in the late 1950s, alone in her Williamsburg apartment while my mother was out of the house and singing on network television, and Grandpa Phil was working at his furniture store down the street, supplying most of his neighbors and Sister Redempta's orphanage with the mundanity of life—the dour mahogany beds, chairs, desks, tables that reeked of utility and plainness. It's Christmastime and I imagine that Gaga's Italian neighbors have decorated their windows with wreaths and tinsel, and tied balsam roping around the banister from the ground floor all the way up to the roof. Sweet, yeasty clouds of baking panettone slither out from beneath her neighbors' doors, and Mrs. Lambiazi who lives two flights below her comes up to borrow extra egg whites for the torrone she's making for her son, who is coming in from Providence with his new wife and baby. By the twenty-third, Gaga tells me thirty years later, the building begins to smell like a fish market: her neighbors are making baccalà and scampi and fried eel, and there's so much pounding and chopping and shouting in Italian going on in the other apartments that she turns on the radio to calm her nerves, and sits down at her kitchen table to listen, alone, and hears, for the first time, The Little Drummer Boy.

Gaga longs to cook great, immense holiday meals that her family—her four sisters and their husbands and children, her own daughter and husband—will love and look forward to every year. But her sisters have scattered, some to Florida, some to New Jersey, and her daughter is afraid of food and starved herself to lose weight so that she could be on television; her husband can't keep weight on no matter what she feeds him and treats food like the fuel he pumps into his Plymouth. So Gaga makes her weekly chicken soup, and her weekly blintzes, and her weekly brisket as if it was nothing more than a chore. It is eaten by her, by her husband, by her daughter, mechanically, angrily, on the run, and entirely without pleasure. Gaga finds her peace and contentment, instead, in the thrice-weekly, middle-of-the-day trips she makes to Leroy Street in Greenwich Village, to see her beloved lady friend Norah; Gaga cooks what she knows Norah loves, and they'll be together through the afternoon, drinking strong tea and sometimes sherry, until Gaga has to take the L train from Fourteenth Street all the way east through Manhattan and across the bridge back to Williamsburg, before Phil comes home from the store, before anyone even knows she's been gone.

Christmas swirls around Gaga, and it sucks her in; over the years, she's come to love it, to live vicariously through the goodness of it, through the noise and the food and the psychic heart nourishment that she so desperately longs for. In Brooklyn, the holiday doesn't care whether she is Jewish, and neither do her neighbors: Christmas climbs the steps of her apartment building and creeps into the rattling radiators and the pipes, and when Mrs. Lambiazi shows up one Christmas Day carrying a pan of steaming lasagna Bolognese, meat and cheese together, and Gaga says, "Thank you, but I can't," Mrs. Lambiazi tells her in Italian that she is now family—Tu sei la nostra famiglia—and that it comes from her home and her heart, and that she must. And so she does. There are only three Christmas songs that Gaga truly loves and will listen to: White Christmas, because it was written by Irving Berlin, and she loves anything written by Irving Berlin; "The Little Drummer Boy," because of its simplicity; and "I'll Be Home for Christmas," which she can't get through anymore without weeping—if only in my dreams—since the morning, fourteen years earlier, when Mrs. Lambiazi got the telegram about her older son who was at Anzio with his battalion. Gaga heard the screaming from two flights up and ran down the stairs to find her neighbor collapsed on the kitchen floor, the radio on, her baccalà still simmering in a pan of water on the stove above her.

If only in my dreams, and Gaga has to take off her glasses to wipe her eyes; once she starts, she can't stop, so deep is her sadness and grief for Mrs. Lambiazi, but really for her own life and situation, and her longing to fill a home with the kind of warmth and laughter and music she'd had when she lived in her mother's house on South Fifth Street, before all of her younger sisters married and moved out and she, at thirty-three, was left behind, and people began to talk.

On this night, in my room in Forest Hills, Gaga sits down on the edge of my bed to watch Bing Crosby and David Bowie sing together, while her latkes fry in a beat-up Teflon pan in the kitchen down the hall, and all she can think of is lasagna Bolognese and the smells of balsam roping and simmering baccalà and sustenance, and life.

7

Motherland

"Y OUR PARENTS SPEAK IN TONGUES," my mother says to my father, as we pull into an empty parking space in front of my grandparents' building.

It's a late Sunday morning in December 1974; I am eleven. And like every late Sunday morning, we have just finished a breakfast of bacon and eggs and the diet white bread that my mother incinerates in the toaster while my father mans the frying pan, which spits angry, sizzling pork fat at him, spattering his wrists with the vengeance of his forefathers. He shrieks with fury at no one in particular and throws the hot skillet into the sink, where he blasts it with cold water and a mushroom cloud of vaporized grease explodes into the air.

We drive an hour out from Forest Hills, rattling along the Brooklyn–Queens expressway and over the rusting Kosciuszko Bridge towards Coney Island, a part of Brooklyn that my father calls the Motherland. I stare out the window at the packed and heaving cemeteries of Queens morphing into manufacturing plants and industrial complexes; I watch as the putrid chlorophyll green canals snake below us and empty into the Gowanus, their surfaces slicked with a soapy rainbow of chemicals, and when I see a tall gas stack with a live blue flame rising from the dank water as if from the bowels of hell, I fling myself onto the musty floor mats of the car and howl in hysterical, pyrophobic terror. My parents ignore me—this Pavlovian response (fire = terror) happens every Sunday—and my father reaches below the heavy front bench seat and hauls it forward so that when I dive to the floor, I have room to huddle for the rest of the journey.

We ride in silence, my mother's white fox coat falling off her shoulders to the crooks of her elbow, like an old-time movie starlet riding in the Rose Parade. She chain-smokes cigarette after cigarette, stubbing them out in the passenger door ashtray until we arrive at 602 Avenue T. On this particular Sunday, my father is seconds away from turning off the ignition when my mother leans forward and pops her new Melba Moore tape into the eight track, fast-forwards it to Time and Love, and cranks up the music. She tosses her head back, closes her eyes, and sings at the top of her lungs, like she's on stage at Carnegie Hall.

My mother has a heavily vibratoed voice that rattles our walls and shakes our parquet floors; she's a belter—a loud, confident, Ethel Merman-ish singer who spent a season on national television and had her own show at the Copacabana in the late 1950s, her volume belying her tiny stature. She and Merman, it turned out, shared both a vocal coach and a decibel level.

"You're the next Judy Garland," the producers in The Brill Building had promised her when she was seventeen, but when a Columbia Records contract was offered contingent upon her touring the country, her parents refused to let her go. There was a season as the girl singer on *The Galen Drake Show*; there were press parties at The 21 Club and The Stork and El Morocco, and the promise of fame. And then there was dating the famous composer Bernie Wayne, and then Thomas, who took her dancing at the Pierre every Sunday, and then marriage to my father, and then a return to Queens where her singing—always loud, always stunning in its power and beauty—was relegated to the cocktail parties of The Marseilles.

"Sing for us—c'mon—sing," the neighbors would say, and I'd watch, my body folded halfway behind a door, as she'd take her place at the front of a living room or a den while chairs were organized around her like an audience. This was my mother—not dowdy and old-fashioned like my friends' mothers—but stunning, a beauty, who made my father the envy of every man in the building. She had a few favorite songs, some of love and some of redemption, always performed as if she was on a stage, alone, under a single, beaming spotlight: "Life Is a Cabaret"; "Bye Bye Blackbird"; "The Shadow of Your Smile," which she only ever sang because it was Buck's favorite request, like she was a singer at a piano bar.

My mother became a stranger when she sang, tossing her head back and closing her eyes in ecstatic bliss. Singing in our living room while I sat on the couch, wedged between Buck and my father, as they drank their scotches while the dog lay at our feet, she emoted from the very depths of her soul. More than once, I cried in fear and buried my face in my father's neck at the sight of her brow, furrowed with drama—I thought that she was hurt and in pain—before I understood that the line between pleasure and sadness was so fine that it was often hard to know the difference. When her song was over and she stepped off her stage, she became my mother again, pouring me a glass of Hawaiian Punch and sending me into my room to watch television. But there's music everywhere, all the time: there's Peggy Lee playing on my father's Garrard turntable when I come home from school, Cass Elliot on The Tonight Show while I'm trying to fall asleep across the hall from their bedroom, and today, Melba Moore on the eight track in my father's Buick.

"Let's GO—" my father shouts to her over the music, shutting off the engine. He gets out of the car, opens the front passenger door, and waits for her on the sidewalk while I stand behind him, holding my guitar case in one hand and a slim green and red book titled *Classic Tunes of Christmas Cheer* in the other.

"I don't want to see them anymore," she says, holding her hand out for the car keys.

My stomach plunges to my ankles.

"But my mother made lunch—" he says. I can see narrow cords of blue vein popping up in his neck.

"Whatever she's making," my mother answers, "I don't want any."

She looks out the windshield, straight ahead, at the car parked in front of us.

My father gives her the keys; she doesn't know how to drive, but it's bitterly cold out and she'll freeze sitting in an unheated car, even in her fur coat.

My mother's sudden display of independence lands like a guided missile at the feet of its intended target; she has forced my father to choose between seeing his aging parents from the old country, or leaving them behind and taking her where she wants to go, back to the new, modern world, where she is woman, hear her roar.

"Please come upstairs, Ma," I whine, bending down to talk to her face to face. "It's Christmas!"

I think of *The Brady Bunch*; Mrs. Brady never threatened to stay in the station wagon on a visit to her in-laws.

"We're not Christians," my mother says, staring out the window. "I'll wait here. You go with Daddy."

My father grabs the sleeve of my new fluffy gray rabbit coat from Bloomingdale's and ushers me up the steps into the lobby, where the gamey odor of schmaltz wraps around me like a boa constrictor as we step onto the elevator and head upstairs.

Grandpa opens the door and looks past us and down the empty hallway.

"Nu?" he says. "So vhere is she?"

"Not hungry," my father answers, and my grandfather shakes his head and waves us in.

FOR A LIFETIME OF LATE Sunday mornings, before we drive out to the housing developments my father represents on the wealthy North Shore of Long Island, my parents and I make this trip to Brooklyn, and I am required to bring something along—some sort of putative accomplishment to show off to my father's parents, an obnoxious totem of my success, like a chapter book I've just learned how to read at the age of six, for which everyone halfheartedly applauds, or my guitar, which I began playing at four. One March Sunday, I carry out a sheaf of handmade Valentine's Day cards fashioned from cherry red construction paper haphazardly pasted over with doilies.

"Vus es duss?" my grandfather asks, unfamiliar with the tradition of Saint Valentine.

On another visit, I proudly show them the paper snowflakes I've deftly avoided cutting up the middle. My grandfather holds one up to the light, squints at it, and laughs while I tell him about my new Flexible Flyer, on which Gaga drags me around The Champs-Élysées Promenade. Or meeting Santa at The North Pole Village on the seventh floor of Macy's, where an elf with a handlebar mustache and a voice like a lady picked me up under my armpits and plopped me down on the fat man's lap.

"Dahlink," Grandpa says, putting his age-pocked hands on my bony little red-sweatered shoulder, "vere I come from, vinter means freezing to death. The Cossacks sent you to the North Pole, and you know what you got there? Gornisht."

These are my Sunday afternoons with my father's parents: a car crash of old and new worlds, of schmaltz and Mitch Miller, of Santa Claus and the Cossacks. My mother locks herself in their ancient bathroom, its old beige enema bag suspended upside down from the shower nozzle, and spends an hour reapplying her makeup while I play show-and-tell until my bored grandmother decides that it's time to eat, and we gather at the kitchen table set with small bone china luncheon plates and glasses of amber SweeTouch-Nee tea. My mother emerges from the bathroom with a new face; we sit down together and she spends lunchtime in silence, rolling around the ice cream scoop of chopped liver and onions, the dollop of Matjes herring, the small ball of sweetened Galician balik fish—boiled chicken dumplings made by poor, landlocked European Jews with no access to or money for actual fish—on her plate silently. My grandmother pours everyone tea; my parents drink it down, zip me into my coat, and we leave.

But today, my mother has decided to stay in the car.

I turn to look back at her when my father and I step into the elevator, just long enough to see her reach over to the ignition; her eyes are closed and her head is pitched back, and I can see her lips moving on the soundproof stage that is our Buick: Nothing cures like time and love.

WE SIT IN THE DARKENED living room before lunch, and my grandparents mumble to my father in Yiddish. He responds in Yiddish while I sit on the couch, kicking my feet beneath the poster-mounted print of Bruegel's *The Harvesters*, which bends and pops out of its rococo frame, concave with the humidity of half a century of damp Coney Island summers.

"Perform for Grandma and Grandpa," my father commands. I unzip my vinyl guitar case and tune it up while I pick out familiar words from their conversation: kinder, and a broch, and a nishtikeit, and tsuris, and chaleria. The baby. A curse. A nobody. Trouble. Evil woman.

I pluck a full, six-string e chord and my father and grandparents look up.

"Play us a song, sweetheart," Grandpa says and I open my music book to my new favorite Christmas carol—the one with the fancy, minor chords that have taken me hours to master—and I begin to strum.

"You have to sing it," my father says, "or we won't know what you're playing."

I blush. I say no.

My mother is the singer. I can't sing. I don't sing. I won't sing. They'll compare me to her; they'll laugh.

"Sing it, dammit," my father shouts and so I begin, playing the introduction before I sing with a shaking voice.

God rest ye merry, gentlemen
Let nothing you dismay;
Remember Christ our Savior
Was born upon this day . . .

My grandmother stands, takes the guitar from me, rests it on a chair, and steers me to the kitchen table, which is set for five. Her white-and-gold-flecked house slippers squeak on the waxed linoleum floor as she putters around me in an apron embroidered with apples; she picks up one of the place settings and dumps it—napkin, silverware, and all—into the sink.

She pads over to the walnut china cabinet where she keeps her good tea set and pulls out a plate. I hear her bang a glass container on the drain board, and then a thwack. She spoons something out onto the plate, tapping and scraping.

"Vy vould she drive out vith you if she didn't vant to see us?" I hear my grandfather say.

"I don't know, Papa."

"Makes no sense. She said she vasn't hungry? She doesn't eat anything anyway. Like a boid."

My grandmother reaches over me and puts down a small, gold-rimmed plate dotted with magenta petunias, upon which is perched an entire brain the size of my father's fist. She touches my shoulder; she hands me a salad fork.

"Ess, honey—it's delicious," she says, before trundling back to the sink.

I stare at the plate; my napkin is folded in my lap. I'm certain I'll vomit: my breakfast will come up. I look down at the brain; it looks back, with its cool gray fissures and swirls, its light pink blood spots shimmering in the afternoon sun streaming in through the window, past the fire escape.

I want to scream, to run into the living room and out the door and down the stairs and out to the car where my mother is having a cigarette and listening to Melba Moore. I want Gaga; I want Gaga's familiar food—latkes, and goulash, and chicken soup. I don't want the brain. The brain. Get the brain away from me.

"Whatever she's serving," my mother had said as we climbed out of the car, "I don't want it."

I remember this while I stare at the brain on the plate.

She knew.

My mother knew.

She knew that we would all sit down to lunch, and on this delicate Austrian china that was dragged over on the boat from Czernowitz with her mother's Shabbos candlesticks, my grandmother would feed us whole boiled brains the day after my parents have taken me to see *Young Frankenstein* at The Ziegfeld where there were brains in glass jars and a man with a moving hunchback and bulging eyes.

"The baby doesn't eat brains yet," my father says, walking into the kitchen with my grandfather.

Yet?

My father's hands leave invisible contrails of the bacon we had for breakfast as he grabs the plate out from under my stare and carries it to the drain board, where it sits like another guest for the rest of our visit. My grandmother curls up her lip in irritation at her youngest grandchild's bad manners, obviously learned at home. She produces bowls of chicken soup, followed by cold balik fish covered in a thin layer of tan gelatin, powdered hot cocoa poured over kosher marshmallows, and thimble-sized shot glasses of Schnapps.

My mother is sound asleep in the front seat when my father and I emerge through the lobby doors and down to the sidewalk; her full pack of Virginia Slims has been smoked and the butts are smoldering in the ashtray next to her. The car battery is dead.

8

Camp

DEPENDING ON HOW YOU SPELL IT, Machanayim means two different things: spelled without a "y," it's the name of a group of
early-twentieth-century Russian Jewish Zionist refuseniks—Jews
not permitted by Russian law to emigrate to Israel—who gathered
together in darkened basements and alleys to study the Torah under
threat of certain death. Spelled with a "y," it is the name of a type of
Hebraic dodgeball, the goal of which is to pummel members of the
opposing team until they relent. Unlike regular dodgeball, when you
get struck with the ball in Machanayim, you're not out: you're simply
conscripted to the other side, where you're pelted by your own former teammates.

Created by a rabbinate who thought they made a pun,
Machanayim-the-Torah-scholars and Machanaim-the-athletes were
pasted together to become the name of an ultra-Orthodox socialist
sleepaway camp for the athletic progeny of Brooklyn Jewish immigrants. In the late 1920s and 1930s, Jewish children were sent off
in droves to a remote part of the Catskills to learn how to play base-

ball like Hank Greenberg—known to his fans as The Hebrew Hammer—to be assaulted with dodgeballs, and to be fed the same foods that they ate at home. Instead of s'mores, children at Camp Machanaim ate schmaltz on rye bread while singing songs around the roaring campfire that licked the starspangled borscht belt sky.

My grandparents sent my father to Camp Machanaim for the first time when he was nine; away from the noise and bustle of Brooklyn and my grandfather's violent rages, he was finally free and at peace, and he learned to love the lush country as an oasis that gave him space to breathe and think. The boyish mischief that made his father apoplectic with fury and resulted in the beatings that inevitably followed at home were met at camp with little more than an extra half hour of sweeping in preparation for his bunk's daily inspection; the mundane naughtiness of a small child was just that, and nothing more. And so my father grew to love his summers at Camp Machanaim, and he longed for them during the cold harsh winters that fell in between. So obsessed with his experience that the very name Camp Machanaim showed up like a regular dinner guest at our apartment in The Marseilles, peppering my parents' infrequent television-laced conversation over the strains of *Beat the Clock* and Tony Orlando and Dawn.

"Way back, when I was at Camp Machanaim—" my father would begin.

When I was at Camp Machanaim . . . What I ate at Camp Machanaim . . . I learned to swim at Camp Machanaim . . . the girl I kissed at Camp Machanaim . . . I learned to be an adult at Camp Machanaim . . . My father's face softened and he beamed when he told me the stories of his bucolic summers away, and I loved listening to them while my mother sat on the other side of the table, pushing her food around in circles and rolling her eyes.

"Well, you're not at Camp Machanaim anymore, are you?" my mother would say, cutting him off.

• • •

A FEW WEEKS AFTER CHRISTMAS break—after Gaga had taken me to see the Baby Jesus lying in his manger at St. Patrick's Cathedral; after Neil Taub's big brother got his head stuck in the cherry red football helmet that my father had given him for Hanukah, wrapping it in blue and silver paper and sticking it underneath his Catholic mother's green aluminum Christmas tree—Candy and I were on the bus heading back to school when she announced that Eugene and Marion had decided that it was time for her to grow up and go to sleepaway camp every summer, beginning with that one.

"So," Candy said to me, setting her Partridge Family lunchbox down on her tightly clenched knees, and tossing her long blond braid over her shoulder, "are you going to keep going to that baby camp?"

Baby camp referred to the day camp that Candy and I had attended every summer since were six years old. A green and white school bus showed up at 7:30 every morning at the top of The Champs-Élysées Promenade and onto it we climbed: Stuey Steinman, Neil, Candy, and I, dressed in white uniforms. We would arrive in prim Roslyn, Long Island, the bus dumping us out onto thick, green Protestant lawns like a pile of gravel, for a day of sack races, kickball, swimming lessons in an overly chlorinated pool; the sort of arts and crafts that involved Popsicle sticks fashioned into jewelry boxes dripping with glue, which the youngest camper, at four, tried to eat; and a daily lunch consisting of the same, mushy boiled food service hot dog served on a bleached white bun, a pint of lukewarm milk, and a lightly bruised apple. We returned to The Champs-Élysées Promenade just before dinner, to mothers who had spent their days sipping too much Soave Bolla out of waxed Dixie Cups while floating around the Fountainbleu swimming pool on their inflatable chaises, dragging their suntanned hands through the cool water; we came home exhausted, filthy, often bleeding, and reeking of the vomit that chronically carsick Stuey Steinman spewed forth every day without fail, on both legs of the trip.

Pressed and ironed Candy Feinblatt had had enough. Candy's cleanliness was the stuff of legend around The Marseilles; her powder blue bedroom was spotless and dusted to a high sheen. Beneath her simple, sturdy wooden bed lay an outsized, imitation antique Oriental rug that Eugene and Marion had found on sale at Macy's, and which gave the space the feel of a bedroom in a high-ceilinged Upper West Side classic six. Candy's Hebrew schoolbooks sat in a place of honor, on her dresser, next to her great-grandmother's monogrammed sterling silver vanity set. Tucked into her dresser mirror was a photo of Bobby Sherman she'd sent away for from Tiger Beat magazine, signed:

To Candy, The neatest girl I know! Love, Bobby xxoo

"He said I was neat!" she cooed excitedly when the photo arrived, clutching it to her tiny chest.

"How would he even know?" I asked, looking around her immaculate room.

"Being tidy pleases God," Candy told me once, when she came over to play at my house. She walked into my room, stopped dead in the doorway, scanned my three-shades-of-pink lair, and gasped. Yesterday's clothes over my desk chair. Piles of books on every surface. A classical guitar propped up against my Radio Shack record player, on top of which teetered a short stack of forty-fives, ranging from The Archies' "Sugar, Sugar" to Olivia Newton-John's "I Honestly Love You" which I played over my headphones every night after my parents went to sleep, swooning at the doe-eyed singer's message, which I was certain was meant specifically for me. A year earlier, my mother's maid, Mary, who cleaned for us once a week from the time I was an infant, stole a baby camp picture of me and had it blown it up to a poster so huge that the resolution bitmapped my face and eyes and made me look like a giant thumbprint with hair. It was Scotch-taped to the wall above my flowered headboard; it peeled at the edges, its tape yellowing and caked with dog fur.

Candy stared.

"Being tidy pleases God," Candy had said, and I longed to please God, to please anyone. Leaving baby camp would be the place for me to start.

"I'm going to Camp Towanda," Candy whispered to me that morning on the school bus, as though she was dangling membership to Skull and Bones in front of me.

In just a few months—if my parents agreed—Candy and I would be leaving behind vomiting Stuey, Popsicle-stick boxes, and undercooked hot dogs, and looking to our future as tidy, devout young Jewish women who were clearly mature enough to begin the separation from our parents. For their part, our parents would have an entire eight weeks of glorious freedom—freedom, I supposed, to do whatever sorts of things parents suddenly unencumbered from the neediness of their sticky, whiny children might do in the throbbing 1970s.

That night, I waited until we were all at the dinner table to make my announcement. Gaga was parceling out flaccid spears of canned asparagus and paprika-dusted portions of fillet of sole wrapped around fake crab, which the local fish market had recently begun carrying under a sign declaring it FANCY AND KOSHER, when I decided to make my move.

"Candy," I said, poking at my sole, "is going to sleepaway camp this summer. It's called Tow—"

I had barely gotten the words out of my mouth when my father leapt up, nearly tripped over the dog, grabbed the kitchen phone, and called Eugene Feinblatt. He dug up a pencil, scribbled down a phone number, and disappeared into the bedroom, leaving my mother and Gaga staring at each other over their plates. Ten minutes later, he was back at the table, glowing with pride as though it had been his idea all along.

"Tomorrow night," he said, puffed up like a fugu, "the owners of Towanda are coming over to show us a slide presentation so that we can see what their beautiful camp is all about. They have inspection and sports and services on Friday nights, and Olympics at the end of the season, just like at Camp Machanaim."

"And the food?" Gaga asked suspiciously, while I sat there, silent. "Will she also be fed like she's in the Army?"

"It's kosher-style," he answered, "and the head chef comes from Yale. So it's not exactly like she'll starve."

Gaga folded her arms and glowered.

Kosher-style. Kosher-anything. I heard kosher, and I envisioned the Feinblatt kitchen, the two sets of dishes and the two dishwashers, and Peggy-the-neighbor, who came over to switch everything on during Shabbos. I imagined my father's parents, and the brain on a plate. But at Towanda, kosher-style meant that milk would never be served with a meat meal and we'd never see a cheeseburger, a pepperoni pizza, or chicken paprikash, or have bacon with our eggs. Instead, meals at Camp Towanda involved pepper steak, veal patties, fried chicken so remarkable that I would go on to dream about it in the depths of the winter, jars of Bac-Os presented with our omelets, and on Shabbos, London broil with small boiled potatoes and thick mushroom gravy. The closest we got to treyf at camp would be the Slim Jims we would line up to buy from Maryann, the blond, blue-eyed snack bar girl at the local bowling alley, sneaking them back into our bunks by stuffing them down the sides of our tube socks.

The next night, ten minutes into a slide presentation shown by Mr. and Mrs. Samuel Nordan of New Rochelle, New York—teachers during the school year; camp owners during the summer and known to scores of children for decades as their beloved Aunt Lynne and Uncle Sam—my father wrote a check for eight weeks away and stuffed it into Uncle Sam's jacket pocket.

THE TRUNK ARRIVES, and then the camp uniforms show up: six brown and gold T-shirts. Six white collared shirts for Friday night services. Six pairs of voluminous, pleated brown shorts. My mother has offset the camp's official clothing list with her own additions: two pairs of denim elephant bell-bottoms from her favorite boutique, hemmed eight inches so they hang over my blue suede Olaf Daughters clogs, and three see-through silk voile blouses and a stack of tube tops in every color that are meant to go underneath them instead of my training bra. Gaga spends every day watching Mike Douglas and hand-sewing name tapes into balls of socks and piles of underwear and T-shirts and three red, white, and blue Speedo bathing suits with modesty panels. My father and I walk around our local Army-Navy store: we select a heavy-duty, water-resistant lantern, an official camping soapbox, a collapsible plastic drinking cup, bottles of bug spray and calamine lotion, and a capacious navy blue rubberized cotton raincoat designed to be worn over a Marine backpack, which falls somewhere between my knees and ankles.

"Cy," my mother says when he makes me model it for her, "she's going to Pennsylvania, not Vietnam."

"She needs to be ready for anything," he answers, rolling up my sleeves.

I begin to wonder whether they are really sending me away for good, rather than just the summer. The clawing anxiety I've experienced for as long as I can remember when I'm about to be left somewhere hits me like a two-by-four, clinging to my back like a drowning man hangs on to his rescuer.

I dream of being stuck at camp, after all the other kids go home at the end of the summer.

I dream of coming off the bus, climbing down the steps, and not having my parents there, waiting to bring me home.

I dream of floating on clouds, high above the earth, of being in limbo, unsure of where I am supposed to be, or live. And then falling backwards, down and down, through the air, out of control, with nothing to grab on to.

And then, she left. She left.

But she came back.

It's too late to back out now, even though my stomach aches and groans for days and something bitter and acidic burns from my belly up into my throat, and my father declares my nerves to be natural, a part of the run-up to a first summer away from home. Candy Feinblatt and Camp Towanda are going to turn me into an adult—a muscular, immaculate American Jew who knows how to fold my clothes properly, say Shabbos prayers in Hebrew and actually understand what I'm saying, eat kosher-style food, and please God with the compulsive neatness that daily inspections will require—whether I want to go, or not.

The afternoon before I leave, my mother packs my lunch in a brown paper bag as directed by the camp's ten-point list of instructions. She wants to make me the usual water-packed tuna with mayonnaise on untoasted diet white that she sends me to school with almost every day; I want Underwood Deviled Ham. "Where did you hear of such a thing?" Gaga asks, looking up from her ironing.

"On television," I say.

"You don't even know what deviled ham is," my mother says, sighing.

"Neither do you," Gaga answers her, folding my camp shorts. "Come to think of it," she murmurs, "neither do I."

But because no Jewish mother or grandmother has ever said no to a food request made by her child, Gaga shuts off the iron, grabs her purse, and marches down Austin Street to the Associated grocery store. She returns ten minutes later, with a kosher pumpernickel raisin loaf and a single, paper-wrapped can of Underwood Deviled Ham, which she places on the kitchen counter. My mother peels back the paper, pops open the can, and sniffs it the way she did my father's Spam; she makes a scrunched, dramatic face, spoons the entire can out onto the bread, spreads it with a butter knife, slaps the other piece of bread over it, and wraps it in tin foil. It sits in the fridge overnight where the meat congeals into salty, porky spackle.

The next morning, the Feinblatts, my parents, and Gaga stand smiling and waving while Candy and I, wearing our uniforms, climb aboard the camp bus, and bid baby camp goodbye forever. The bus driver's transistor radio, hanging off the rearview mirror, blasts "Maggie May" while we near the resort town of Dingmans Ferry; we open our identical brown paper sacks, spread small napkins on our laps, and extract our sandwiches—Candy, her sturdy and predictable peanut butter and jelly; me, my Underwood Deviled Ham on pumpernickel raisin—and take simultaneous petite bites. When she is done, Candy meticulously pats the corners of her mouth with her napkin before rolling her bag up and awaiting the arrival of the garbage counselor to come marching up the aisle; when I am done, I pat the corners of my mouth with my napkin, roll up my bag, and am instantly and violently ill.

YEARS LATER, WHEN I'M A teenager, my parents both separately tell me about their first summer alone, while I was busily ensconced in the Camp Towanda dining room, standing at attention in my camp clothes for meal-time prayers, and filing into the camp social hall for Shabbos services. My mother got shingles the minute I climbed onto the camp bus. She tells me that after she recovered, she and my father attended a Friday night fondue party where my father was handed a tightly rolled joint, and fearing certain arrest by one of the cops of the 112th Precinct down the street from The Marseilles, he got up and flushed it down the toilet.

My father remembers that the fondue pots that suddenly appeared on every coffee table in The Brussels and The Marseilles that summer—white-on-brown Dansk saucepans that hovered over a small can of jellied Sterno; sets of long, two-pronged forks meant to skewer hunks of meat or bread to be dunked into bubbling gruyère—were purchased not for cheese, but for keys.

He says that Pammy, the divorced hippie neighbor from The Brussels, who, after seeing Billy Jack, strolled around The Champs-Élysées Promenade dressed in a soft, goatskin poncho the color of caramel and strings of love beads, her long braid in a suede sheath, had the first "fondue" party shortly after camp began. All the neighbors, their kids away, gathered at one apartment; upon arriving at said apartment, the men dumped their house keys into the fondue pot, which would be sitting on the coffee table. Every woman in the room, assuming they were playing, picked up a two-pronged, long-handled fondue fork. Every woman, when it was her turn, stirred the pot and fished out a set of keys. "The man belonging to the keys," my father explains to me, "gets serviced by the woman."

He says it like it's normal, like he's relaying instructions for building a bookcase: place Part A into Part B. I imagine horses at a stud farm.

"What do you mean, serviced?" I say. "You know—" he says. "They shtup."

I can see Marion Feinblatt, shaking her head, not getting it; she probably tells Pammy that it's Shabbos, but beyond that, the fondue simply cannot contain beef—she and Eugene can do chocolate or fruit or bread, but they can't mix their cheese and their meat—and declines the invitation. Richard and Laura Steinman attend, as does George Hoffmann, whose wife and boys have already left for Denmark. Velma and Buck have sent Darleen off to a camp for physically disabled children, and they arrive, Buck in snug powder blue Sansabelt trousers and Velma in a filmy peasant blouse because the weather is so warm. I can hear Neil Sedaka singing "Love Will Keep Us Together" on the stereo in the background, and they all sit around the coffee table—some on the floor, some on the couch, some pull chairs over from the dining room— and when the keys are dumped into the fondue pot, Velma, who hates sex anyway and has been dragged to the party by her husband who accuses her of being antisocial, excuses herself and walks out to the terrace where she chain-smokes Parliament menthols while Buck's keys are deftly and immediately fished out by Pammy, who has been trawling the pot with a long, royal blue–handled fork. They disappear into the bedroom to catcalls and whistles and shouts for more hors d'oeuvre from the kitchen. Pammy has made a special treat for the occasion, stuffing pitted Medjool dates with a tender, raw almond and wrapping them in single strips of bacon. They bake until the meat sizzles and crisps and drips thick, smoky, unctuous fat into the toothsome fruit and onto the sweet, young nut.

"These are Devils on Horseback," Pammy tells everyone with a wink when she sets them down on the coffee table. "Help yourself to more."

"Did you ever play?" I ask my father.

"Of course we didn't," he answers gruffly, annoyed that I would even dare to imply that my parents might have been anything but on-lookers, too cool to care.

That first summer, Candy and I and two hundred other campers closed our eyes in silent, peaceful prayer before every meal, as sets of keys were fondue-forked by polyester-clad parents we knew from the school bus stop and the dry cleaners. We stood at attention in a brown-paneled dining hall in rural Pennsylvania around fifty tables laden with meat meals or dairy meals, for prayer—devotions in Hebrew followed by English, led by Uncle Sam and Aunt Lynne or the Anglican British counselors they hired to care for us every summer. From the youngest camper of five to the oldest camp worker of seventy, Jewish children and Anglican counselors alike, we bowed our heads and spoke words thousands of years old.

Baruch atah Adonay, Eloheinu Melech Ha'Olam Hamotzi lechem min haaretz.

Blessed art thou, oh Lord, thy God, who bringeth forth bread from the earth. Amen.

Pammy brought cookie sheets of hot bacon-wrapped stuffed dates out to the twitchy, nervous guests in her living room; one hundred miles away, we lit Shabbos candles in the camp dining room. We finished our London broil dinners and moved silently into the social hall on chilly nights, and to our campfire ring when it was warm enough to sit outside under the stars, just downwind from the kitchen's exhaust fan, which blew gusts of beef fat into the air around us.

Long, narrow fondue forks hunted and scraped for keys and coupled neighbors who recognized each other from parent-teacher conferences and school plays disappeared into bedrooms while the sun set around us in the hills of northeastern Pennsylvania, and a kind-eyed, soft-spoken older man we called Uncle Sid, who acted as our resident rabbi, led us in the prayer that would stay with me forever and that now, forty years later, I will whisper to myself on a bitter Friday night in New England while I am walking the dogs, the snow crunching under my boots. I say it to myself as a balm, as a way to still myself, my mantra.

Dear God, as the sun hangs in the western sky and the hills cast lengthened shadows, a spell of quiet comes over our little world. There is a calmness on our lake and the heavens are reflected in the water. The rustling of the branches in the trees is hushed and a stillness settles over camp and in our hearts. Thy Sabbath has come. We cease our many activities so that we can think of those things that make worthwhile our coming together in play, in sport, and in comradeship. Open our hearts so that we may allow Thy Goodness to enter.

Eight weeks away.

I learn sleepaway-camp Hebrew by rote; I sing the songs and say the prayers like I understand every word. When we pray in English, we ask together, two hundred of us at once, in a drone that wraps itself around me like a blanket, which steadies my mind and turns off the anxiety spigot:

How can we know God? Where can we find him? He is as close to us as the birds and the trees, and He is as far away as the hills in the sky. He causes the winds to blow and the rains to fall, and speaks to us in the music we hear and sing. That is how we know our God—through the goodness that passes before us. He is in our acts of kindness; he is in our joys.

I sit next to Candy on a splintering white-painted bench in the camp fire ring and gaze up to the vast, sapphire sky and breathe in peace. He is in our acts of kindness; he is in our joys, I repeat to myself. I believe that, finally, I have somehow found what Candy has found, without Miss Kranowitz and studying the Haftorah.

BROWN AS A RAISIN FROM the constant sun, thin and muscular from being in perpetual motion for two months, I step off the camp bus in the odiferous Bay Terrace Shopping Center parking lot, the Cross

Island Parkway roaring along a few blocks away. The night I came home, I stood on our screened-in terrace, facing The Brussels and The Champs-Élysées Promenade. My father slipped Binky's collar on and met Buck downstairs to walk the dogs while my mother disappeared into the bedroom. School would be starting in two weeks.

He is in our acts of kindness; he is in our joys.

The late summer air was sweet and dank—a steaming blend of honeysuckle and cement and garbage piled up behind the building near the garage.

What do you want me to make for your return? Gaga had written to me, two weeks before I came home. *I'll make it for you, special.*

Despite the heat, Gaga made me Hungarian goulash and served it to me in an earthenware bowl like I was the Queen of Sheba herself. She reached over my shoulder and ladled it out of a large, brown-and-white wooden-handled saucepot I'd never seen before, its underside stamped with the name Dansk.

"Welcome home, Elissala," she said tenderly. "Now, honey, ess."

9

Sylvia

MAGNIFICENT, OUTSPOKEN, IMPERIOUS Sylvia Gerson, my father's only sibling and older than he by five years, remained unconvinced.

Camp, she was certain, would keep me a child forever, and shackle me to an unacceptably long adolescence that would, in turn, keep me from the one thing that every young woman needed to focus in on like a laser: marriage.

When she learned that my parents were continuing to send me to Towanda deep into my teens, she was like a dog with a bone. It didn't matter that I had, thanks to the fastidious Candy Feinblatt, discovered the importance of prayer during my summers away, and partook of a summertime kosher lifestyle despite the presence of treyf in my life everywhere else I turned.

"But where will it lead? You're wasting time and you're wasting money," Aunt Sylvia warned my father, days before he and my mother packed the car for visiting day. Sleepaway camp, according to Aunt Sylvia, was frivolous at best: expensive, shallow, and, in her estimation, enabling children to grow up without any kind of responsibility or sense of obligation to their future. It was fine, she said, for children to spend summer at camp for a season or two at most; then, they should be expected to partake in more serious cultural pursuits leading to social advancement and, ultimately, conjugal bliss. Her own children had each attended sleepaway camp for a few years before I was born, but the bulk of their summers were spent at the Woodstock, New York, family compound, which was built by Sylvia's architect husband, Lee, and his architect father, in the late 1940s as a way to get the family children out of the city during one of the worst polio epidemics ever recorded.

There, beneath the shady elms of the legendary artist's colony, where Will and Ariel Durant wrote their eleven-volume *The Story of Civilization*, Aunt Sylvia and her husband's family spent their summers in cultivated bliss: they read, they knitted, they needlepointed, they played duplicate bridge, they did the *New York Times* crossword puzzle in ink, and, having been denied admittance to the then-restricted Woodstock Golf Club, they joined the Kingston Country Club just a few miles away. Sylvia was a consummate hostess, and her summertime cocktail parties were the stuff of delicious legend: there were games on the lush lawn between the compound's three houses, homemade blueberry pies, her mother-in-law's famous kosher potato knishes made with Nyafat, and extravagant, French-style towers of prawns presented on a three-tiered silver brasserie-style platter. A sliver of pork in any form never touched her lips or entered the confines of her home, but prawns, boiled gently and served with wedges of lemon and cocktail sauce, were Sylvia's gateway drug, and a nice big fuck you to the Woodstock Golf Club and its boatload of so-called liberals, and just about as far as she could get from the schmaltzladen two-bedroom apartment in Coney Island where she had grown up sharing a room with my father.

But camp? Ab-so-lute-ly not.

Aunt Sylvia believed that life for a young Jewish girl of even moderate means was meant to be lived and experienced in a certain methodical and particular manner: there would be dance lessons, drawing lessons, piano lessons, membership to the symphony and the Metropolitan Museum, French lessons, travel to Europe, maybe a teen tour, college at an Ivy, and then, marriage to a Jewish doctor or a dentist or a lawyer. Naturally, there would be babies, a house in the suburbs, and eventually, the country club. Sylvia was a woman with plans and goals and a deep sense of determination, and nothing ever dared stand in her way or say no to her. Everything about the universe she created for herself seemed perfect and effortless and safe. Hers was a world of propriety and conformity and security, and the chaos of my childhood household pushed me into her gravitational field like metal to magnet: I longed for her approval and her acceptance, and was naturally drawn to her, even though she terrified the shit out of me.

Sylvia and Lee lived in a tidy brick house abutting the Long Island–Queens border not far from my father's beloved Golden Ghetto. Not quite a ranch, not quite a split, Sylvia and Lee's home was lushly landscaped—there were boxwoods and hydrangeas and pines tightly planted around the foundation, and fruit trees planted in the backyard, like an English estate. The house was divided in half: up a short flight of thickly carpeted plush steps were the bedrooms—an immense master suite for my aunt and uncle, and two separate bedrooms for their daughters. Uncle Lee didn't believe in bedroom furniture; instead, every room was outfitted with walls of hand-hewn floor-to-ceiling built-in drawers and closets that opened and closed as though they were gliding on silk runners, even in the wettest heat of the hottest summer. The living and entertaining areas were far on the other side, in a vast, arch-ceilinged living room that was as long as a bowling alley and as wide as a barn. In the spotless, modern kitchen, a wall of knotty pine cabinetry sat across from an eat-in breakfast nook, which had a stereo tuner built directly into the wall, so that one could listen to the morning news while eating one's breakfast. There was a marble and onyx Aztec chess set in colors of cream and eggshell that sat, untouched, on a gold silk–draped antique card table at the entrance to the living room. A gleaming walnut baby grand piano stood opposite the chair-railed dining room, its tall, mahogany metronome in the shape of an Egyptian obelisk sat on the piano's lid, quietly tocking the minutes and hours away, softly, like a witness, during the many events that Aunt Sylvia hosted.

SHE WAS—SHE IS; she is ninety-seven as I write this—stunning, statuesque, comely, an Ava Gardner lookalike. As a child, I believed that Aunt Sylvia awoke every morning of her life with her jet-black hair miraculously teased and sprayed and her makeup in place. Uncle Lee, tall, mostly bald barring the narrow strip of gray hair that ran across the back of his head from ear to ear, was never seen in anything less formal than an ironed business shirt, trousers, and leather oxfords. Which is how they appeared when they arrived at Camp Towanda unannounced on a late Friday afternoon just before the camp was beginning to get ready for Shabbos dinner and the outdoor services that followed. One of my English counselors, Sandy, called me down to the head counselor shack, bent down on one knee, held my hands, and told me that some people from home were here to see me. Sandy's eyes filled with tears; the only time family members showed up at camp unannounced and formally dressed was if somebody had died.

"It's going to be okay—" she said through her thick Cockney accent, while I stood there, frozen, still in my T-shirt and shorts, filthy from that afternoon's field hockey tournament. "Whatever happens—it'll be fine," she sobbed, reaching forward and hugging me. "Go on now."

I pulled away and ran up the long road that led to the office and the dining hall, breathing hard as I burst into the small red clapboard building, and let the screen door slam behind me. Uncle Sid's wife, Ruth, looked up from her desk and over to the back porch, unsmiling.

"Your Aunt Sylvia and Uncle Lee are here to see you—" My aunt and uncle were sitting on the porch's ancient, painted Adirondack chairs, Uncle Lee in his pressed shirt and formal shoes, Aunt Sylvia in a denim outfit with silver studs running up and down the seams of her pants, her hair teased high and perfect. She was holding an enormous white and blue gift box from Macy's.

"Hello, Elissa. We just decided to take a drive in the country—" She stood up and thrust the box at me. "This, darling, is for you."

"What's wrong—?" I asked. "What's the matter?"

My parents were on vacation in Europe: A car accident. They were leaving me. They decided not to come home. They don't want me anymore. They're moving. Without me. I'm going home with Aunt Sylvia and Uncle Lee, but not to Forest Hills. Not to Gaga. Not to my parents. Or Darleen or Stuey or Candy or even Inga.

"Nothing's wrong—" Uncle Lee said, smiling. "We just came to see you and to give you a gift. And we'd like to take you out to dinner in town. Someplace nice."

Dinner in town. Someplace nice.

Sweat rolled down the small of my back and into the damp waistband of my shorts.

I stared up at them; they stared down at me.

Saying no was not an option; no one ever said no to them—not my father, not my mother, and certainly no one who was not yet an adult. No—a polite declining, a rejecting, a refusal of any sort— was a defiant betrayal, an act of disloyalty so egregious that it landed errant, boundary-drawing cousins on the outer periphery of the family forever or kicked out wholesale, never to be heard from or talked about again, except in a faint whisper, as though they were dead. Dinner in town, someplace nice after a spur-of-the-moment, two-hour drive to rural Pennsylvania from Long Island felt final.

I HAD ONLY BEEN ALONE with Sylvia and Lee on one occasion: in 1966, when they strolled out of my parents' Thanksgiving dinner after coffee and pumpkin pie with my three-year-old self perched on Lee's broad shoulders.

"Want to come home with us, sweetheart, to stay?" Aunt Sylvia whispered to me in our foyer while my parents were in the kitchen, cleaning up. She bent down so that we were eye-to-eye, threw her mink over her shoulders and beamed a broad smile.

I coyly shook my head yes and was instantly scooped up, aloft and barefoot, in my pink Tinker Bell nightgown. Uncle Lee carried me down the hall on his shoulders, where the three of us waited in silence for the elevator to arrive; it arrived, we got on, and the door slammed closed behind us.

"Duck your head down, honey," Uncle Lee said holding my bare ankles, as we stepped out and into the lobby. The other elevator door rattled open, my father flew down the marble steps that led to the promenade, and grabbed me backwards off Uncle Lee's shoulders from behind. The trip back upstairs to our apartment with my father is a blackout; suddenly, I'm in my bed, my safety railings have been pulled up, and Gaga is kissing me on the head and tucking my sheets around me so tightly that I can't move, like they're four-point re-straints.

Years later, at a family gathering in the Midwest—long after the divorce, after Uncle Lee died, after my own father was gone—I will catch Aunt Sylvia watching me work in my cousin's kitchen, helping prepare dinner for ten of us: roast chickens and steamed broccoli drizzled with garlicky vinaigrette and smashed sweet pota-toes. Younger cousins chopping, cooking. Laughter. I am on the inside; safe. She beckons me over to where she's sitting, on the marble fireplace surround overlooking the living room, where half a dozen small children are playing a board game on the floor at her feet. I wipe my greasy, chickeny hands on my apron, and walk over to her.

"What?" I ask, bending down. "Do you want some water?"

I love her, although I've never told her that, nor has she ever told me. I want her to love me back; I still long for her approval the way I did when I was a child, and the safety of her inner circle. I kneel in front of her, genuflecting as though I'm in church.

"No, darling," she says, unsmiling. She grabs my hand. "But I want you to know something."

She pauses.

"I wanted you. To have you."

I stare at her and blink. Her coiffed black halo has gone a softer, warmer brown now that she's in her nineties.

I stand up. I push my hair back off my face with my free hand. She doesn't give up the other one. I struggle to breathe. My knees are fighting to keep me upright; I struggle to keep from crawling inside myself, to that familiar place where I can't hear anything or see anything, where the world around me goes black. Time coils back on itself; the decades slam shut. It could be 1966. Or 1974. But it is not; I'm almost fifty now, living my life. Safe.

"I was worried what you'd become in that house," she says. "Did I do okay?" I ask.

"I'm not sure," she says.

I pull away gently. I smile and go back to the kitchen. Aunt Sylvia was brilliant, and perfect. Her children were brilliant, and perfect. The home she shared with Uncle Lee was controlled and neat, and without the chaos that swirled around our Queens lives like a tornado. There was no shouting, no rage, no fondue pots clanging with keys, nothing unexpected. Everything was planned; scripted; completely predictable. Every woman in my father's family, young or old, aspired to be Aunt Sylvia, to be just like her: to throw parties like her, to dress like her, to act like her. To be her.

Except for Gaga and my mother.

"A groyser gadilla," Gaga would say, rolling her eyes. A big deal.

I LOOKED OVER AT RUTH, who smiled and stood up from her desk. "That's lovely that you'd like to take her out, Mr. and Mrs. Gerson, but tonight is Shabbos, and Lissie is leading some of the prayers at services. You're welcome to stay and join us—I'll call the dining room and you can sit at the head table with me and my husband, and the Nordans. But Elissa is not allowed to leave the property with anyone but her parents."

"Lissie is leading special prayers at Shabbos services?" Aunt Sylvia said.

"She is," Ruth said, "isn't that right, Elissa?" I nodded; it was news to me.

"Well, that's quite all right—" Aunt Sylvia said, putting her hand on my shoulder. "We won't stay—but Lissie, why don't you open the nice gift that Uncle Lee and I brought for you all the way from New York?"

I set the box down on the broad arm of one of the Adirondack chairs and carefully opened it; I pushed back the white paper lining the box. Inside it was tucked a zip-front, triple-weave housecoat with an enormous, pointed collar. It was meant for a middle-aged woman, and was thick and weighty and covered in jewel-toned Sumatra lilies and delphiniums and orange ranunculus.

"Take it out," Aunt Sylvia commanded. "Let's see if it fits."

I pulled it out of the box and it unfurled like a red carpet; I held it up to my chin and the bottom hem pooled on the floor of the camp office, half a foot beyond my sneakers. It was the sort of formal loungewear that one wore as a guest staying at Aunt Sylvia's home. If they were forty.

"Put it on, for heaven's sake!" she said, exasperated.

I unzipped it from neck to knee, and began to step into it. "Over your head! Come now, Elissa—we don't have all day! We have to get back—"

I stepped out of it, picked it up from the bottom and pulled the housecoat over my dirt-caked, Queens College T-shirt and nylon gym shorts, my red-striped tube socks, and my dusty suede Adidas Gazelles. I had to bend down to zip it up.

"It's simply beautiful," Aunt Sylvia cried, clasping her hands together. "I wish your daddy could see you in it. Give us a hug goodbye."

I padded over to them, trying not to trip. I gave them a hug goodbye, flowers of sweat starting to bloom under my arms. Aunt Sylvia and Uncle Lee thanked Ruth, and off they went, just as quickly as they had arrived, down the main camp road to the parking lot, into their Lincoln, and home.

Ruth and I stood in silence, side by side at the office screen door, and watched them drive away as the waiters began to place scuffed plastic pitchers of bug juice on every dining table in preparation for the arrival of Shabbos, and our Friday night meat meal.

10

Prayer

THE DAVENING BEGINS just as the sun is coming up.

The minute the first light shoots beams through my eastfacing window—I can see the mottled, hazy outlines of the empire State Building, the Chrysler Building, the new Citicorp Tower with its oddly slanted roof in the distance—Moishe Garbfeld clears his throat and chants the morning prayers: the Shacharit, the Shema, the Amidah. I lie in bed, half asleep, half dreaming, in a gray, negative slip of consciousness. Staring at the ceiling, I place my hand on the bedroom wall I share with Shaina Garbfeld. I can feel Moishe's rumbling, weeping drone of devotion as he prays in her bedroom, facing east towards the city, and Jerusalem, while she stirs and the day begins.

Fear of God, Moishe chants from the ancient Hebrew Psalm, is the beginning of wisdom.

MOISHE, JUDITH, AND SHAINA GARBFELD keep to themselves. I have spent almost fourteen years in and out of neighbors' apartments, and they ours; the only way I know there is someone living on the other side of my bedroom wall is when I hear Moishe daven every morning for an hour before he leaves for his job in the diamond district. Every day, he prays when the sun comes up; he is still praying when my father returns from walking the dog and heads into the kitchen to make our breakfast, while I dress and my mother showers and puts on her makeup. Strange, unfamiliar odors slither out from under the Garbfelds front door, permeating our hallway—years later, I will recognize them as olive oil, garlic, lemon, tomato, and toasting cumin that to me smells like exactly like sweaty armpits. Judith is making something that I will come to know as Israeli shakshuka: eggs cracked into simmering, cumin-laced tomato sauce and then run under the broiler; they will sop up the silken yolk with warm pita bread. When Moishe reaches the part of his morning prayer where he beseeches God to help save him from the bad influences he may encounter during the day—May it be your will to protect us—my father and I are sitting together in our kitchen, eating our cremated rashers of Oscar Mayer bacon and dry scrambled eggs overcooked to the consistency of an asbestos mat. My father passes me the ketchup and I whack the bottom of the bottle, and it bursts all over my plate in a crimson explosion.

On the other side of the wall, I imagine Shaina and Judith are putting their plates in the sink while Moishe unwraps the worn leather straps of his tefillin down the hall in Shaina's room. He unrolls his sleeve, puts his jacket on and then his hat, walks out of the apartment, and runs into my parents, who are late and heading into the city for work: Mosaic, the English-language, secular cultural Jewish magazine my father has launched with my mother's old boyfriend, Thomas, is failing, and my mother has returned to her former life as a fur model after nearly fifteen years of being a housewife.

IT IS 1977 and our closest friends have moved away in droves:

Inga and George Hoffmann have rented another, larger place in a distant part of Queens. Eddie has transferred to a school in another district and Tor is back in the hospital near his parents' new apartment, trying to kick the heroin that he buys from a married lady in The Marseilles; he shows up at Inga and George's last cocktail party wearing a blue bandana like Jimi Hendrix, to cover up the track marks that dot the vein running down the middle of his forehead like a cord. Candy Feinblatt is attending a special high school for gifted students in Manhattan—she will make it to MIT in three years, when she's seventeen—and Eugene and Marion have moved to a small condo in the city so that Candy can spend her time studying instead of commuting. Buck and Velma have quietly packed up Darleen and the Chihuahuas and left for an unnamed town on the South Shore of Long Island.

"They have to leave," my father tells me when a moving van shows up one morning and we see their electric fireplace being hoisted onto the truck; word has spread along The Champs-Élysées Promenade that Buck's deep and loving affection for children, particularly little girls, has become a problem.

My after-school hours are spent locked in my bedroom alone with my twelve-string guitar and the albums that Gaga buys for me at Sam Goody in Manhattan when she makes her thriceweekly trips into town to visit Norah, her lady friend, who she has secretly loved for more than sixty years. Gaga comes home with Michael Martin Murphey's *Blue Sky–Night Thunder*, and I lie on my bed wearing massive brown Koss headphones, singing "Wildfire" at the top of my lungs until Gaga barges in with a plate of hot matzo meal latkes with apple sauce; I contemplatively fingerpick John Denver's "Rhymes and Reasons" over and over again until my hands ache. My schoolmates are listening to early disco. I'm out of step and out of sync; I'm an outlier and a loner, and with my parents leaving for work before I go to school every morning, I dress myself, which thrills my teasing schoolmates and teachers alike: my friends point and laugh at my fake cowboy shirts with gingham yolks and pearled snaps. My teachers point and whisper at my stiff unwashed Wrangler jeans that I wear with enormous Western-style belt buckles the size of silver platters. I walk home alone from school every day wearing a floppy brown leather hippie hat with a braided lanyard that hangs down my back; one morning, I open the coat closet door to look for it and it's gone, like my father's shearling coat.

"I might have seen it someplace," my mother says when I ask her about it. "But I couldn't possibly say where."

The next day, after school, she meets me at the front door in her mink jacket—she's left work early; it's a special occasion—and tells me to leave my coat on; she takes me shopping to her favorite boutique for the clothes she loves to see me wear: transparent voile blouses, tube tops, the Jordache jeans that are so tight that I have to lie down on the dressing room floor just to zip them up.

"You just have to lose some weight," she says, tugging so hard at my zipper that her face reddens. On the way home we stop at the drugstore and she buys two boxes of caramel-flavored Ayds diet candies; she leaves one on top of the stereo in my bedroom, and the other underneath my bottle of vitamins in the kitchen, where I can't possibly miss them.

MY FRIENDS AT SCHOOL ARE having sex. Marcus Goldberg was recently sent home from eighth grade for showing off a chain of dark purple bruises around his neck, a gift from Lily, a new girl at school, half Chinese, who has moved here from San Francisco. At fourteen, Lisa Epstein has lost her virginity to Stuey Steinman in the guest bathroom during Neil Taub's birthday party; her mother takes her to Manhattan and has her fitted for a diaphragm, which she proudly exhumes from the depths of her green canvas knapsack while on the school bus, gingerly prying open its beige plastic case and passing it around for show-and-tell.

"Don't drop it!" she cries, and we all handle it like a baby bird, examining it under the sunlight streaming in through the bus windows, while Neil's boom box sits on his lap, blasting Bohemian Rhapsody.

I pretend to be interested in Lisa's tiny round of rubber, and in the package of pills that Lily passes around the next day, which she says she takes every morning with her daily chewable vitamin. I achingly lust after something I can't name; I know, instinctively, that it needs to be hidden. There's a slow burn that sometimes happens below my navel, like the striking of a match, when I see Karen, the seventeen-year-old lifeguard from the pool attached to The Marseilles; she's so quiet, so soft-spoken that I have to strain to hear her say hello. She wears a woven turquoise surfer bracelet, flat leather sandals, no makeup, and her thick brown hair pulled back in a loose ponytail held in place by a fat red scrunchie, which she pulls off and puts back on all summer, whenever she's nervous. The September night before the pool closes for the season, I offer to help her stack the lounges and do one last skim; we listen to America sing "Don't cross the river if you can't swim the tide" while we work, and when we're done, she orders a pizza from across the street and pays for it with a wad of cash pulled from her jeans pocket. In the dusk, we sit together cross-legged near the cement edge of the pool, and eat in silence, hot orange pizza grease dripping down the front of our slices onto the aquamarine concrete. Karen lives on the other side of Queens Boulevard and goes to school in a different district than I.

"Too bad," she says quietly, folding a big, triangular slice in half, New York–style. We say goodbye and she gives me a warm hug; she doesn't let go first. I think about her all year; I don't even know her last name. Six months later, in the middle of winter, I'm waiting in the bitter cold to cross Yellowstone Boulevard around the corner from the Tung Shing House. For some reason, I'll never know why, I look up as the Q60 city bus drives by, and there is Karen, sitting in an inside seat, resting her head against the window. She turns toward the street, puts her palm on the glass, and smiles. I pull off my ski glove and hold my hand up and smile back, as if sending code, and the bus careens by.

During Aunt Sylvia's formal sit-down Thanksgiving dinner for twelve that year, my father pulls me and my cousin Sarah into my uncle's darkened, book-lined den. Older than me by twelve years, Sarah will spend every one of Aunt Sylvia's holidays with me huddled in a corner, from the time I am a young child: she will read to me and talk to me for hours, while the party swirls around us.

"Tell her what colleges you want to visit next year," he says at me.

I sit down on the loveseat in the long, green crushed-velvet skirt and the high-necked, puffed-sleeve, ruffle-front blouse he has bought for me at Macy's; all that's missing is a bustle.

"Well," I say, "Mount Holyoke, Smith, Wellesley, Wheaton, Goucher."

"That's great," Sarah says. "How nice! Wonderful women's colleges, all of them."

"My grades aren't very good," I say, "so it's just stupid." I study the basket-weave pattern on the carpet.

"You won't know until you try, though," she says. "Right?" We both smile and look over at my unsmiling father, whose face is reddening; he loosens his tie.

"We have determined," my father announces formally, as though I'm not there, as though I have vaporized in front of them, "that Elissa is heterosexual."

A wave of nausea creeps up my legs; my knees feel like Jell-O. "And how, exactly, did you determine that?" Sarah says.

He is tongue-tied and can't answer. He abandons the conversation, defeated, and laughs nervously. He leaves us alone in the den together.

"Let's get some air," Sarah says, standing up. "Dinner won't be done for a while."

We put on coats and hats and she deposits her year-old daughter in a stroller and we leave the house. We walk my aunt's tidy suburban neighborhood in silence, street after street, up hills and around corners, down the block to the highway entrance, past rambling 1960s ranch houses and massive, landscaped colonials with streams of cars parked in their driveways. We walk back in stillness, even her small baby has fallen asleep, and we open the basement door, which leads to my uncle's office; we slip inside and remove our hats and coats, and skulk back up the stairs into the living room, past the walnut butler's table and its resident silver tea set, the family photos from Woodstock on every shelf in every room, and the Greek Key silver on the dining room table set for twelve, and no one has even noticed we were gone.

In Forest Hills, Lisa Epstein is losing her virginity and passing around her birth control on the school bus for all of us to gawk at, and Suzi Quatro has replaced Olivia Newton-John on my childhood turntable, and the leather-clad bassist stares back at me from the cover of "Your Mamma Won't Like Me," which I keep buried in my closet, behind my guitar case. All winter long, I write to my coltish English counselors from Camp Towanda, sending them flimsy aerogram letters to places called Hertfordshire and Devon, truly believing in the recesses of my sloppy teenage brain that they will remember me. I am certain that this is my secret, this separateness, this difference that I feel grinding at my core, as real and mine as a fingerprint, forbidden as failure.

"Don't go near the gym teacher," my father says to me after a parent-teacher conference at my school. "I don't like the looks of her—" he adds, pulling his snuff tin from his pocket. "You know what they say."

My face is pocked with the weeping ravages of teenage hormones; I spend hours sitting in a chair at Garren at the Plaza, the most expensive salon in Manhattan, where my dark blond hair is chemically, violently straightened on demand by my mother—my scalp is burned and singed and I bite my lip to keep from weeping— when all the girls show up at school with silky tresses blown out like Farrah Fawcett. Two weeks later, after repeated shampoos and swims in the heavily chlorinated Forest Hills Jewish Center pool, my entire head inflates to a wide triangle of frizz under the stress of humidity and chemicals. She drags me off to a dermatologist who spends a full hour jabbing my swollen, aching face with hypodermic needles packed with acne medication; when I fight her on it—it's not working and it hurts so badly that tears run down the sides of my face into my ears during every procedure—she bursts into the examination room, all bluster and shouting, held back by two nurses who have grabbed hold of her arms as if she's in a barroom fight, to make sure

that I'm not giving them any trouble. She stocks the medicine cabinet in the bathroom I use with makeup—mascara and eyeliner and
lip gloss in a color called Perty Flirty—as a hint.

She says, "Try. Just try. For me."

My passions are Karen whose last name I'll never know, and
Suzi, and Camp Towanda. He is in our acts of kindness; he is in our
joys, I whisper to myself every Friday night after dinner during the
winter, reciting the bits of Sabbath services that I can recall while I
fall asleep to strains of Dark Side of the Moon coming through the
wall I share with Shaina Garbfeld.

THE DOORBELL RINGS on a late Friday afternoon; I open it and there
is Shaina, looking like Marie Osmond in her Paper Roses days, with
cascading waves of thick, dark brown hair that roll down her back,
almost to her waist.

I sometimes see her getting on the elevator in the morning to
meet the private bus that drives her to the yeshiva she attends in
Douglaston, half an hour away. Dressed in a navy blue melton coat,
prim white blouse, and dark serge skirt that falls well below her
knee, Shaina stands out the way I do amidst the green snorkel parkas
and orange burnished Frye boots that everyone is wearing. She neither talks to me nor smiles.

"She's frum—Orthodox—" my father tells me one night over dinner. We're eating a sausage pie from the pizzeria downstairs; I've
been complaining that most of my friends have left the area. Maybe,
I think, Shaina wants to be friends.

"She's only interested in God," he says, taking a long drag off his
cigarette, "like your grandfather. Save yourself the trouble." His
words come out through a haze of smoke.

I chew on a pizza end and pout.

"She has nothing to say to you, Lissie—" my mother adds, her
voice clipped with exasperation. "Make friends with the kids at your
school. And stop already with the crust—" She reaches over, takes the
end of the pizza out of my hand, and drops it on the floor for the dog.

On the afternoon that finds us facing each other in the hallway, Shaina introduces herself to me through a thick, wet lisp; heavy metal braces are clamped to her teeth like bear traps, top and bottom, connected with small rubber bands. Home from yeshiva for the day, she is barefoot, dressed in old Levi's bell-bottoms that have tattered to soft blue strings around her painted toenails. A Bonne Bell cola-flavored Lip Smacker hangs off a black cord around her neck. She pushes up the red sleeves of her baseball shirt to reveal the same braided sailor's bracelet that I wore all summer in camp until it blackened, rotted, and fell off on the bus ride home. "I really like your guitar," she says, her hands on her hips.

"You play great—"

"How do you know?" I ask, my arms folded protectively, looking at her feet.

"I can hear you through the wall—" she laughs, tossing her hair off her face. "I can hear everything!" She winks and cracks her gum so loud that the dog barks.

"Jewish girls don't chew gum like cows," I remember Gaga saying to me once. Well, I think, this one does.

Shaina can hear me—my music, my laughter, my angry sobs after my father's rages, my youthful groans—the way I can hear Moishe beseeching God every morning.

I spend every day after school in Shaina's apartment, until my parents come home from work. Judith sits in the kitchen reading People, while we disappear into Shaina's bedroom, its pineapple yellow–painted walls covered in earth-toned macramé hangings that she and Judith brought with them when they moved here from Israel after the war in 1973. The minute she walks through the door, Shaina sheds her yeshiva outfit like a snake sheds its skin, replacing it with snug elephant bell-bottoms and tight black concert T-shirts emblazoned with Kiss and Tommy and Emerson, Lake, and Palmer. She piles up a stack of records and arranges them on her stereo pin and Judith barges into her bedroom without knocking and sets down a platter of toasted pita bread torn into small pieces and drizzled with olive oil and sesame and sumac, which makes the sides of my tongue hurt.

"You'll stay for dinner," Judith tells me, unsmiling as she walks out of the room.

I sit at the Garbfelds' heavily carved dining room table creaking under the weight of alien foods I've never seen or eaten before: stuffed grape leaves, roasted eggplant dip, tabbouleh, and round, deep-fried balls that, until I bite into them—they're my first taste of falafel—I believe are meat. My mouth, unaccustomed to the bitterness of the garlic and crushed fava beans and eggplant and chickpeas mashed to a thick paste, aches. Moishe and Shaina and Judith eat in silence; she killed her first Nazi at seven, and now, she's feeding me dinner. I wonder if kindness can flow from the same fount as brutality, if the two are somehow mutually exclusive. There is no talk of boyfriends or fashion or what Shaina will or won't do to get into a good college; there is no talk at all.

There is just food, and eating, and sustenance.

"Sit," Judith says to me that night. She points at the table. "Eat."

IN A CORNER of her bedroom, at the spot on the wall between us where it meets the floor, Shaina, who loves to draw, has begun free-hand painting with the acrylic paints that she keeps in an old Tretorn sneaker box under her bed. Her mother knows about it, Shaina says; Moishe sees it every morning while he davens. In quiet moments after school while I lie on her floor, playing my guitar, Shaina paints a little bit every day: it starts with a small brown primordial soup that seems to emerge out of the brown shag carpet itself. A week later, emerald green lily pads sprout from its depths, balancing on narrow stalks like scrolls; eventually, tiny frogs will crawl up and out of the soup with outsized, Lewis Carroll eyes, and long, unfurling, flicking tongues that wrap themselves around the daisies that Shaina has painted growing on the shore. In a month, there will be a bright red toadstool flecked with yellow spots perched upon a thick, penile stem, and everywhere, flat, green cannabis plants with pointed leaves in threes, fives, and sevens.

It's an early Friday night when Shaina feigns illness and begs off services; with Judith and Moishe in shul and my parents at a movie,

she decides that her masterpiece is complete and insists we celebrate.

"Let's have a cocktail!" she lisps, her hooded brown eyes brim-
ming with pleasure. My heart races in my chest so hard and fast that
my gingham cowboy shirt, untucked from my jeans, flitters against
my skin. Before I can say no—do I even want to say no?—Shaina
leaves me sitting on her bed and returns with two azure blue goblets
in one hand and a can of Coca-Cola in the other. Wedged under her
armpit is a half-empty bottle of Manischewitz Heavy Malaga procured from the depths of a living room cabinet. She struggles to
unscrew it—sugar has congealed around the screw-top cap, sealing
it like cement; it's thick and syrupy and gives off a familiar, warm
cloud that smells like Grandpa Henry's apartment in Coney Island.
She pours it expertly into the glasses from on high, like a bartender,
and tops it off with fizzing splashes of soda, and hands me a glass.

Shaina the devout; Shaina the frum.

Shaina, who, I will learn over the next three years, rolls the tightest joints, acquires the best hash, buys the strongest quaaludes,
drinks the darkest rum, and fucks the most yeshiva boys, takes me
by the hand and pulls me down onto the shag carpet in front of the
toadstool and the mucky pond and the perfectly rendered cannabis.

This Shabbos night, we lie on our backs and slur along to Cher's
"Half-Breed" on the turntable. We have one glass and then two and
then three; we get drunk on the profane swirled together with the
wine of ritual, and for the first time, the world around me seems
warmer and kinder. Shaina and The Marseilles and Cher spin around
me as I put my hand on the wall that separates our lives—it lands
someplace between the mushroom and the sludge, between beauty
and filth—and I throw my head back, close my eyes, and belt it loud,
like my mother: Both sides were against me since the day I was born.

PART II

How far must you go back to discover
the beginning of trouble?

—PHILIP ROTH, *Epstein*

11

Officer's Mess

H E HAD BEEN SO HANDSOME—a catch, everyone said: blond and blue-eyed with a soft, sad brow, a kind mouth, and a pouty, winsome face. It broke his heart to leave his mother in Novyy Yarchev, he told me when I was a little girl. Even back then, as a child, I couldn't fathom it: how does a twelve-year-old boy pack himself up and run away, across a continent, across an ocean, by himself?

"What did you take with you?" I wanted to know. "What did you carry?" I sat on his lap one afternoon at Aunt Sylvia's house, mystified by his story. He smiled and pointed to the ceiling. I looked up at the crown molding.

"Hashem," he said, closing his eyes in a reverie and letting his hand drop to his chest, over his heart.

Hashem, he believed, would protect him wherever he went and whatever he did. Hashem would guide him and direct him; Hashem would provide his moral compass and be his anchor.

Once he got settled, after he landed his first job setting hot lead type for the Yiddish newspaper *The Day*, my grandfather devoted himself entirely to pleasing Hashem, who, he knew in his heart, had looked after him on his journey to America. He studied the Talmud daily, learned English, found love, and became, as he liked to say, a regular Yankee Doodle boy.

By early autumn of 1944, Grandpa Henry looked like the American he longed to become: he is dressed like an Edward Hopper character, in a conservative herringbone tweed overcoat and his favorite dark wool fedora from the JJ Hat Center on Fifth Avenue. Years after he dies, I find this very picture of him long forgotten in a torn Klein's of New York shopping bag buried deep in his hallway closet, tucked in among ancient, dog-eared photographs and old, gilt-edged Hebrew yahrzeit calendars sent over from the old country before the war; my grandfather gazes away from the camera at something unseeable, perhaps into a hopeful future, or a past filled with regret. This pose will become a trademark of virtually every family photograph; each one of us, without exception and regardless of age, glances away from the camera, as though we'll surely turn into pillars of salt like Lot's wife if we make direct eye contact with time.

On the day my father comes home on leave from the Navy, my grandfather stands solemn and pensive, I imagine, waiting for his youngest child outside the civilian pick-up gate at Floyd Bennett Field, a crumbling Yonah Schimmel potato knish in one pocket and a rolled-up copy of *The Day* in the other. He had left work early that afternoon and headed out east to pick up his son, the aviator, who was flying himself home after receiving his wings in Corpus Christi. As a twenty-one-year-old night fighter pilot in the U.S. Navy, my father still didn't know how to drive a car and, like a teenager, needed a lift home.

My grandfather munched on the remnants of his beloved knish— until the day he died, his regular treat after filing his social page stories—pointed his chin to the sky, and waited for the sound that my father told him to listen for: a low, dull thunder, a steady roar that would grow louder and stronger with his son's approach. I can feel the aching, sudden homesickness that overtakes him—it happens when he least expects it; it runs in the family and wraps itself around me like

a shawl, and like him, I find myself yearning for a past that was sometimes violent—and lodges in my grandfather's throat like a wad of
guilt; it had been so long. He himself had forgotten where home was,
what it looked and smelled like, and what his mother's kitchen tasted
like: the Friday night cholent cooked for hours so that it would be
ready in time for Shabbos dinner. The autumn borscht, and the stray
ropes of sinewy flanken peeled in long strands off the week's boiled,
disintegrating bones and folded into misshapen purses formed from
hard winter flour and water and whatever broth his mother could afford to use. He could smell it as he stood there waiting for my father
in the Brooklyn seaside chill, running cold knish crumbs through his
dry fingers and shaking his head, his eyes suddenly filling with tears.

Ach, he sighs from someplace primal, like an animal.

The little news he got about the Ukraine wasn't good: the last
time he had heard from his mother was in 1938. A postcard. She said
that she was staying put in their little town because, she wrote in
Yiddish, what would anyone want with a little old lady in the middle
of nowhere? I'm insignificant. Small beans. Bupkus.

My grandfather paces back and forth, thinking of his mother and
the autumn borscht of Shabbos dinner. Standing at the airstrip, he
remembers the last thing she told him before he ran away: "No matter where you go, Hirsch, remember Shabbos, and keep kosher." If
only she could see him and his family now; if only she could see. If
only she had left Novyy Yarchev when she had the chance, before
the Nazis came.

It will be seven years before he learns of his mother's fate: he will
find a distant cousin from his shtetl, resettled in a Boston suburb.
My father drives him there and hears the story: the Germans didn't
want to waste diesel fuel on such vermin, and executed every resident in the forest outside the town. The cousin himself was shot in
the back and left for dead; he will live for the rest of his life with a
hump. At the telling of the story, my grandfather leaps to his feet in
this tidy suburban living room not far from Walden Pond and beats
his long lost cousin bloody, so profound is his grief; they never see
each other again.

On this day at the airfield, I imagine my grandfather staring down at the nice wingtips he's begun wearing since he's been doing a little better at the paper; he takes off his hat and runs his index finger down the top crease. He sets it back on his head and waits for his son to blast through the sky like Superman, the radio hero who always saves the day against the most impossible odds.

MY FATHER TAKES OFF FROM the Naval Air Station on Cape Cod, traveling south along the coast of Rhode Island and Connecticut before reaching New York, where he heads west, out over Boerum Hill. He banks hard to the right and then loops back, swooping down over the synagogue roofs and the kosher butchers and my grandmother's favorite fishmonger, who has sold her three pounds of fresh carp for the gefilte fish she's made for my father's arrival home. He turns his plane east, out over Ocean Parkway, grazing the treetops and the low-rise apartment buildings, lining up 602 Avenue T in his crosshairs like a beloved target. Lightly, tender as a caress, he squeezes the locked trigger on the gun sight.

Boom, he whispers.

In Brooklyn, he is still known among the neighbors as Henry and Bertha's little Seymour—my grandmother will call him Shmuel, pronouncing it Schmeel, to the day she dies, which drives him crazy—who'd rather play stickball and listen to Audie Murphy on the radio than say his prayers. He's the little Seymour with the funny sense of humor, who loves to make people laugh, who loves the special foods that his mother makes just for him; he's the little Seymour who will hide from his father's violence beneath the carved legs of his mother's Knabe baby grand, the lilting Chopin Études she practices each afternoon punctuated with the sounds of rage. Music, perhaps, is a form of genetic memory, a heavy cloak of protection against a family anguish so ancient and deep that it has seeped into my grandfather's, my grandmother's, my father's, my own corpuscles. Through the generations and over the arc of a century, we listen to Chopin's Opus 10, no. 3—Tristesse; sadness—on the radio, or at a young cousin's first piano recital, and separated by time and circumstance, it binds us together like the color of eyes. Every member of my family weeps when we hear it; none of us knows why.

Aunt Sylvia's husband, Uncle Lee, is stationed in France with the Army Corps of engineers, chasing the Germans east after the Allied landings; Sylvia and her new baby, my cousin Maya, are living with my grandparents until the war is over. My father has told them precisely what time he's going to fly over the building, and they race up the echoing hallway stairs from the fifth floor to the sixth, throwing the roof door open just as he's passing over. My grandmother waves a schmaltz-caked flowered kitchen towel and my father spots them, small as ants, and salutes them by dramatically tipping his wings, before heading off to the airfield.

My father strafes Ocean Parkway every time he comes home for leave, right up to the end of the war in 1945. The Navy offers to bring him back to New York on a troop plane, but as long as he has wings and is in uniform, he wants to fly himself to the airfield, less than five miles from where he grew up.

AS A CADET IN 1943, my father gets the same three meals a day, every day: farina for breakfast, chipped beef on toast—

SOS, or shit-on-a-shingle—for lunch, and an unidentifiable meat with a canned green vegetable and a boiled potato for dinner. There are endless cups of watery coffee. "Saltpeter," his friends tell him, "is in everything from the ice cream to the hamburgers, so don't even try." No one asks him if he has any dietary restrictions he must abide by lest the God of his Fathers rain down hell upon his head. For the first time in his life, he can eat what he wants, when he wants, however he wants. Everything is a temptation; he trembles with guilty, thrilling delight at the thought of breaking the rules everywhere from the mess hall to the whorehouses that his squadron frequents if they have even a few hours' leave.

On August 1, 1943, he writes to my grandparents from preflight school in Del Monte, California:

. . . I have a deep feeling in the job that must be done. For the crusade against evil to be successful, every fighting man must feel the spiritual support of his loved ones behind him. To you, I am still the blonde boy, naughty at school, with all the faults. But you must think of me as an individual whose job is to train to kill your enemies and then return, without having lost the teachings of his parents, home, and religion in the process. . . .

Tucked into that letter is a newspaper clipping entitled "A Mother's Prayer," by syndicated columnist George Matthew Adams, which is reprinted in America's newspapers during the holidays:

God, Father of Freedom, look after that boy of mine, where he may be. Walk in upon him. Talk with him during the silent watches of the night, and spur him to bravery when he faces the cruel foe. Transfer my prayer to his heart.

Keep my boy inspired by the never-dying faith in his God. Throughout all the long days of a hopeful Victory, wherever his duty takes him, keep his spirits high and his purpose unwavering. Make him a loyal friend. Nourish him with the love that I gave to him at birth, and satisfy the hunger of his soul with the knowledge of my daily prayer.

He is my choicest treasure. Take care of him, God. Keep him in health and sustain him under every possible circumstances. I once warmed him under my heart. You warm him anew in his shelter under the stars. Touch him with my smile of cheer and comfort and my full confidence in his every brave pursuit.

Fail him not—and may he not fail You, his country, nor the mother who bore him.

"Vuss es duss?" I imagine my grandfather mumbling as he reads the prayer. Devout Jews don't ever print or write the word God on anything that is considered impermanent or that can be thrown away; instead, they write G-d, with a dash. He hands it to my grandmother, who reads it again: she never prays for her son in this stilted, inauthentic manner with its unique form of sanitized, movie-script American zeal and its unfamiliar Christian phrases. Still, she tucks the clipping into the pocket of her flowered apron and reads it over and over, pleading with God—somebody's God—to hear her and return her Schmeel to safety. She folds the prayer back into my father's letter and slides it into the depths of a drawer in the hallway table where it will remain untouched and forgotten until I discover it one Sunday morning in 1991, the year after my grandmother's death.

MY FATHER BECAME AN AVIATOR—Ensign Altman, Lieutenant Junior Grade—on a blisteringly hot day in August at the Naval Air Training Center in Corpus Christi, Texas. The next day, August 3, 1944, he wrote to his parents in stiff, shaking cursive:

> *Right now, I'm living in the Bachelor's Officer's Quarters and boy, is it snazzy. This being an officer is really hot stuff. Everybody salutes. I've got to be immaculate (shave twice a day). Meals are all very formal. Waiters in white mess jackets, heavy silverware, beautiful service and linens, and I've got to constantly remind myself not to SCHVITZ.*

I can see my grandmother standing in the kitchen, the windows facing the fire escape thrown open to the Coney Island breezes, reading the letter aloud to Grandpa Henry, who is slurping a bowl of cold, emerald green schav for dinner and laughing at the description of the silver and the service and the meals.

"Just like Ratners—" he mutters, and they both laugh and shake their heads before my grandmother continues to read.

> *I have a huge private room complete with carpeting and mahogany desk, for which I pay thirty-five cents a day, since I'm staying in the status of a visiting officer. There is a colored boy whose job it is to keep my room spotless, make my bed, shine my*

boots, and practically brush my teeth. The Navy has wonderful traditions along those lines since in previous years all Naval officers were of the wealthy aristocracy. So who am I to kick about being treated like a lord?

My grandfather puts his spoon down and looks up from his bowl.

"So now he's a vealthy aristocrat? Let him just come home in vone piece."

And come home he does: on this day in early autumn, 1944, my grandfather, his fedora tipped back on his head, is not prepared for the star-spangled American spectacle that awaits him at Floyd Bennett Field. My father confidently lands his plane and is waved over to the hangar. He pulls open the cockpit cap, reaches over his shoulder for a small, dark green Navy-issue valise, climbs out onto the wing, and slips to the ground. He disappears into the hangar and, ten minutes later, emerges in his mid-weight woolen green uniform, his new wings gleaming like an ingot on his left breast.

"Vow," my grandfather murmurs, as his son steps up to him; they hug, stiffly. My grandfather pats him on the back like a baby who needs burping.

"Velcome home, Captain America," he says, unsmiling. "Your mother made supper, and then ve'll go to shul."

They drive home to 602 Avenue T, where gefilte fish and boiled chicken and potatonik—the special comfort foods of my father's childhood that his mother knows he loves—are waiting for them. They walk down the hallway and the sounds of their heels on the tiled floor and the smells of Shabbos cooking bring tears to my father's eyes in a rush of homesickness and want. When dinner is over, they walk to temple: my grandfather steps onto the bimah to sing the Shabbos services while my father—wearing his yarmulke, his bar mitzvah tallis, and the uniform of a Naval officer—prays for the safety of his nation. Grandpa holds the Torah scrolls aloft by their wooden handles, then rolls them up and slips them into their velvet sheath. His massive, cantorial prayer shawl covers his head, and he lays the Torah on his shoulder so tenderly, like a baby, as he floats up and down the aisles of the airless synagogue, his eyes closed in a meditative trance. He is elsewhere, in a dream; he is a child, running through the dusty streets of Novyy Yarchev. Tears cascade down his cheeks as he passes his son, who reaches forward to touch his tallis to the Torah resting on my grandfather's shoulder. He floats past my father like a ghost.

Three days later, my father flies himself back to Cape Cod, and from there, returns to Corpus Christi on a troop plane. He arrives at the officer's club in time for dinner and watches a rockjawed lieutenant commander sitting at the next table gingerly sip a crystal clear cocktail from a tulip-shaped glass, a small onion nestled in its dimpled notch; my father orders one and drinks it down like cool water, the taste of juniper coating his lips with a surprising burn. The waiter carries over a silver bowl laden with a dozen massive Gulf prawns surrounding a small dish of cocktail sauce; he uses his fingers, chewing down to the fantailed stump of each shrimp. A block of pâté arrives, with a small silver basket of black bread and tiny pickles that look like shrunken versions of the ones he used to pluck from the barrels on Delancey Street. The main course is two thick pork chops, half a rack of smoked Texas pork ribs mopped with spicy sauce, and two obscenely long German sausages, which remind him of the tough, uncircumcised Italian boys in his gym class, and he giggles to himself like a naughty child at the thought. He eats all of it with a combination of rage and fervor; at first, it tastes bitter and alien, but then washes his father's rejection clean and leaves in its place the sweet flavor of acceptance and belonging. He has broken the code and scoffed at the law; he is a Jewish boy dressed in an American Naval uniform, living and eating like the Gentile everyone on base will believe him to be.

Feverish and lying in bed at the base hospital the next day, an IV drip in his arm, my father was covered from head to toe with thick, angry welts of contrition; broken to his soul that his father had again not recognized him, he shed his Levitical virginity like a wounded foreskin, breaking his Talmudic contract over a massive platter of treyf in the officer's club. While the buxom Texas nurses pumped him full of antihistamines they hoped would keep him from blowing up like The Hindenburg, my father slept on and off like the child he still was, dreaming dreams of a grandmother he would never know, toothless and gummy, the words Hashem, Hashem falling from her lips.

Dearest Mother, he wrote when the fever finally broke, *It was wonderful to see you and Sylvia and the baby. I'm writing to you from the base hospital. I am fine, but perhaps I ate something I shouldn't have. Don't tell Papa. Love, Cy.*

12

A Different Sort of Woman

A T THE SAME TIME that my fighter pilot father was flying his Grumman F6F Hellcat off the deck of the USS *Enterprise* in the Pacific, my mother gazed at the mirror and dreamt that she was Ava Gardner, born to southern Catholic tobacco farmers in Johnston County, North Carolina, up from nothing. At seven years old, after seeing Ava's walk-on as a Parisian store clerk in Reunion in France, she waited until her parents were busy with customers in their Williamsburg furniture store, and walked herself down Grand Street to Perretti's Pharmacy, where she dumped her allowance on the counter and asked for a bottle of black hair dye.

"Does your mother know you're buying this?" the druggist asked.

"Yes, Mr. Perretti; my mother knows. And I'll take a lipstick as well, thank you," she said, putting a tube of Revlon Cherries in the Snow alongside the bottle of Clairol Blue Black #124. Trundling home with her booty, she locked herself in the bathroom, lopped off her long mousy blond banana curls with her mother's blunt sewing scissors, and dyed what was left a color that does not exist in nature.

Shortly after the beating was over, Gaga hauled my mother off to one of her four sisters, who owned a beauty shop and had significant experience undoing bad dye jobs.

"Fix it, Blanche—" my grandmother ordered, dumping my mother in a chair.

"If I dye it back, I'm afraid it'll burn. She could lose it all, Clara—"

I am certain, having heard this story over and over again through the years, that Clara—Gaga—considered having my mother completely shorn, had it not been for her firm, undying belief that, ugly or not, a girl's hair is her crowning glory. This belief was handed down like a myth; at fifty, when I finally cut my thin, unruly hair short, my mother didn't speak to me for a week, as though I'd committed an unpardonable sin.

Blanche's husband, Harry, carrying an ivory walking stick and his skin barbecued to a dark cordovan from too much time visiting his family in Cuba, came into the back room where my mother was sitting, weeping quietly.

"Let her hair come back to itself naturally, even if she has to go school with it like that—" he said.

"She'll look like a skunk, you idiot," Gaga groaned.

"It'll serve her right, like a scarlet letter," Harry snarled. He poked my mother hard in the cheek while she cried like the baby she was, simply for wanting to be something that Gaga regularly assured her she wasn't: beautiful.

YOU ARE NOT A MOVIE star, for God's sake," Gaga would say to her little girl, throwing her heavy hands up in disgust at my mother's penchant for spending every last cent she had on Hollywood magazines and makeup, from the time she could remember. "—and we're not tobacco farmers, you might have noticed," she continued, pointing around the thickly draped, mauvepainted living room packed with fancy, claw-footed Duncan Phyfe furniture.

But my mother couldn't be blamed for her fixation on Hollywood and glamour: it was Gaga's fault that her young daughter had become so smitten with the movies and the enthralling tales of other people's lives. From the time she was five, she was deposited at the local Williamsburg playhouse, where she could sit through as many movies as she could stand, emerging blearyeyed after an imaginary romp with Cathy and Heathcliff on the Yorkshire moors, or from Judith Traherne's bedside right after Dr. Steele diagnoses the brain tumor. But after the movies were over, my mother returned home to her unhappy parents: a kind, soft-spoken, gentle-tempered furniture store owner devoted to another woman who happened to be a nun so faithful to him that despite the fact that he was Jewish, she posthumously made him a member of the St. Vincent's Purgatorial Society, where novenas are still being said for him to this day; and a tantrum-prone eldest daughter of a towering kosher Williamsburg butcher who dropped down dead in the middle of making a Shabbos sale, right in front of my ten-year-old grandmother. Practical even as a child, Gaga finished wrapping the fresh helzel for Mrs. Mandel so that the old lady could get her soup done before sundown. "Seeing a parent die like that changes you forever," my father once told me, shaking his head. "It makes you mean."

And perhaps it did. Although Gaga's rage might have had more to do with being what my mother once called a different sort of woman. One by one, her sisters began to marry; one by one, they began to have children. The eldest, she was still single when the last one left and neighbors began to talk. Forced into marriage at thirty-four by wagging tongues and the kind of gossip that could destroy an entire family in the early days of the twentieth century, Gaga fulfilled her conjugal duty exactly once, on her wedding night, and nine months later produced a sallow, somber baby—my mother—who with every day spent in front of a Hollywood movie, suckled on the promise of stardom and beauty as though it was the food of life itself. The sustenance—the love, the comfort—that I found in the kitchen, at the table, my mother would find on the stage, in the spotlight; her saving grace would be the magnificent singing voice she was blessed with, and the lithe beauty she eventually grew into. While I nurtured myself with food, my mother did the opposite, and molded and shaped her body into unnatural svelteness: she grew up to resemble not a single member of the family, as if she weren't even related.

In a black-and-white family photo taken in the 1940s, my mother is wearing heavy, dark, wartime clothes and a knit beanie, her parents perched behind her on the sidewalk in front of their Grand Street apartment building; if the picture had been shot in color, the image would have been the same—dull, gray, devoid of life and warmth. My grandparents didn't tell my mother to smile, and she didn't come by it naturally; even at seven, she looks heavy and tired and big as a teenager, and utterly unlike her pretty and thin cousin Rebecca whose father, Gaga once told me, was a card-carrying member of the Communist Party.

"Just like Edward G. Robinson," she added, nodding.

By nineteen, after my mother has starved herself to bony, skeletal slimness and devoted her life to performing and singing on television, Robinson will lean over to her in a taxi after they leave the Stork Club together, across a haze of Shalimar and the crinkle of black taffeta, and whisper softly in my mother's ear that No, sweetheart, he was certainly not.

GAGA KEPT A KOSHER HOME and served her husband and daughter buttered toast and farina for breakfast, steak for lunch, and every night, a full-fat milchig—dairy—meal: there were cheese blintzes and potato blintzes and mock chicken à la king. There were cheese knishes and cheese pierogi and scrambled eggs, noodle kugels sweetened with sugared farmer cheese, raisins, and cinnamon; there were foot-long cheese strudels and almond horns and babka. After dinner, believing it would keep her daughter healthy, Gaga sent my mother to bed with a glass of warm whole milk, a thick layer of skin floating on the surface like a blanket. Every time, my mother threw it up: drink, vomit; drink, vomit. One night, my mother flatly refused it; Gaga chased her down the hallway with the glass until my mother tripped, fell down the stairs ass over elbow, broke her nose, and couldn't eat anything for a week. She lost eight pounds.

"That," she told me years later, "was the best weight-loss regimen I was ever on. I looked fabulous."

Food, in my mother's life, will become dangerous, forbidden, the devil on her shoulder; it will terrorize and taunt and harass her. As a child, I will find her sneaking Entenmann's chocolate-glazed donuts in the kitchen in the middle of the night; she will inadvertently leave a trail of crumbs that the dog will Hoover up and then barf near my bedroom door before sunrise. And still, when I'm eleven, with the television blaring Tony Orlando and Dawn at the end of the table while my father sips his scotch and reads the *Times*, she will ask me over a dinner of bland fillet of sole wrapped around canned asparagus whether, during the day, I've had any of the special Ayds candies she's left for me on my stereo; she glares at me and waits for an answer. Gaga, who is puttering in the kitchen just a few feet away, has taken on the job of picking me up from the school bus every afternoon; instead of bringing me directly home, we stop off at the luncheonette or the pizzeria, where she feeds me after-school snacks of grilled cheese and bacon, or thick, square slices of Sicilian pizza topped with rounds of pepperoni. My mother doesn't know.

"Eat," Gaga says, sitting on the green leatherette luncheonette stool next to me. "It's good for your strength," she says. "It's good for your heart."

So I eat; Gaga and I keep an eye on the luncheonette door in the tarnished mirror over the soda fountain to make sure my mother isn't strolling in, which she never is. Food becomes our secret; it becomes my sustenance, my love.

While I poke at my fillet of sole, Gaga doesn't look at my mother. When I don't respond to her, she gets up, leaving my father and me at the table, and walks into the bedroom. The box of Ayds candies will remain on my stereo for weeks, on top of The Eagles' *Their Greatest Hits*. It will be like this forever: my mother will imply a weight problem, even though, until I hit puberty, I'm so thin that I'm almost concave. Gaga will continue to feed me on the sly; my father will take me out for secret Saturday afternoon meals while my mother is having her hair done. Piles of *Vogue* and *Harper's Bazaar* will magically show up in my bedroom, strategically placed on my dresser, in front of the mirror.

MY MOTHER HAS BEEN BLESSED with the miraculous voice of a child-angel and will sing for anyone, anywhere. At twelve, she sings "Bess, You Is My Woman Now" with the kind of overwrought, outsized emotion reserved for professional actors twice her age. She sings in the furniture store for my father's customers, and for Sister Redempta; they gawk at her like she's a sideshow and applaud for her as though she's on the stage at Carnegie Hall.

Overweight and glum, my mother summons up another person when she performs, even if just for the mirror: she croons with sad irony at eleven, performing love songs so vivid and tender and completely inappropriate for a child her age, that she seems possessed by the devil himself, for simply longing for the arms of adult love in whatever form it may come. It's as if she somehow knows, from the day she is born, that she is the unintended consequence of marital duty as commanded by The Mishnah; she is a child objectified and rarely loved. Fifty years later, after a flock of psychiatrists can't knock the depression out of her system, she admits to me that she grew up knowing far too much, that living daily with two people prevented by time and consequence from having the lives they wanted, was too much to fathom. She knew about Ken Johnson, who, at fifteen, had kissed Gaga in front of the old Stanford White Madison Square Garden. Ken, a schoolmate, was Catholic and unsuitable for marriage to a young Jewish girl; my grandmother would keep his letters, caked with the mud of the Somme, until the day she died. She retreated, ultimately, into the arms of her beloved friend Norah, until one day Norah had a stroke and no longer recognized her. I came home from school to find Gaga sitting in our foyer armchair, in the dark, her chin on her chest, weeping alone.

Grandpa Philip, married to a woman who didn't love him, devoted his emotional life and affection to the poor Catholic parish down the street, and to feeding, clothing, and providing furniture for

St. Vincent's Home, the orphanage connected to it. When he died, in 1967, he would, according to the mass card that bears his name, share in five thousand masses celebrated each year by Missionary Bishops and Priests; in all masses celebrated at St. Vincent's Home; in a Novena of Masses said each month, and in all spiritual and corporal works of mercy performed by the Home in its mission of charity to the underprivileged and neglected youth committed to its care.

My grandfather had turned his love elsewhere—to the only other woman in his life, Sister Redempta—when Gaga slapped him for trying to make love to her.

They never slept in the same bed again.

"When I met the Sister," he told my father, "it was like I found God."

"Well," my father said, "you sort of did."

13

Captain America

Y OU'VE BEEN AWAY for four years. You owe it to us to stay," my grandfather told my father, on their final drive home from Floyd Bennett Field.

My father had studied celestial navigation in Edmond, Oklahoma; Lawrence, Kansas; Hamilton, New York; and Palo Alto, California. He learned how to fly at night in Pensacola and Vero Beach, and was awarded his wings in Corpus Christi. He had spent the end of the war flying off the deck of The Enterprise at night, in total blackout, landing on the unlit moving aircraft carrier in the middle of the Pacific, without any guidance beyond the stars above him and the plastic celestial navigation charts that lay in his lap. He watched friends crash their F6Fs onto The Enterprise's runway and burst into flames; he watched another friend—the squadron buffoon, "a dope," my father told me—miscalculate his landing, topple off the deck into the water, and drown in his locked cockpit before a rescue crew could reach him.

He came home a man; his parents thought he was still a boy. He wanted to move to California, to attend Stanford on the G.I. Bill;

they said, "No, you owe us." So my father got a job at an advertising agency in the city and studied for his college degree at night, returning to the tiny childhood bed he'd slept in as a young boy. Every night after classes were over, he'd stop at Rolf's on Third Avenue and gorge himself on piles of bratwurst, sweet and sour cabbage, spaetzle, and pitchers of lager. And every night, he'd come home and find his father sitting in the foyer and waiting for him, reading Der Forverts and having a cigarette while his mother was in the kitchen, scouring their milchig dinner plates.

"Maybe," my grandfather said, looking up as his son took off his overcoat and hat and hung them in the hallway closet, "you could possibly have dinner vith us after school, Mr. Big Shot?"

Before my father could answer, Grandpa Henry would sniff, dramatically, like he smelled something foul, like his son had stepped in dog shit.

"You smell," he'd say, "like treyf."

THEIR FIGHTS WERE MYTHIC. They continued every night for one relentless year, beginning the minute my father walked into the apartment after school. There were accusations and arguments, complaints about disrespect and my grandparents' inability to treat my father like a man, fights over who was a real American and who wasn't, and what made a son good or bad, according to the Talmud.

"A good son would stay home with us," they said. "A good son would spend more time in shul. A good son wouldn't come home stinking of pork. A good son would remember where he came from."

"You didn't," my father blurted out to Grandpa Henry one night.

The world around them stopped: a line of rage had been pulled taut until it snapped like a rubber band. My father could hear nothing, he said—not the traffic outside on Ocean Parkway or the clanging of my grandmother's dinner dishes in the sink. Father and son stared at each other from opposite corners of the darkened living room. My grandfather flung a heavy, leather-bound Yiddish edition of Shakespeare's *Henry IV* at my father's head, like Moses hurling the tablets at the recalcitrant Hebrews. It missed my father by inches, struck the end table near the couch, and landed beneath the legs of my grandmother's baby grand, its spine broken, its beautiful gilt-edged pages splayed open and torn.

A week later, my father left; Manhattan wasn't far enough. California, a day away by air, wasn't far enough. Instead, he fled the country entirely; he became someone else living someplace else, crossing the northern border to a place where he had absolutely no connections, no friends from the Navy, no distant family who might call his parents and report on his comings and goings. He took a job in Canada as a road salesman for the London, Ontario–based Knit King Corporation, traveling the length of the country from one end to the other for three years, limiting his trips home to once a month. Arriving on Friday night, he'd eat supper with his parents, and still dutifully attend shul on Friday night and Saturday morning. They'd nudge him to call the shy Jewish girls they deemed acceptable, whose mothers played pinochle with his mother, and whose fathers spent their Saturdays davening in shul with his father; the bespectacled analyst he saw in Toronto told him to placate them rather than fight, that it would just be easier, and so he did. He took the girls out, one by one; he never called them again. On Sunday mornings he'd take a taxi to Idlewild Airport and fly home to his tiny apartment across the border, blissfully alone, living a quiet life that belonged completely and solely to him, devoid of Talmudic obligation and familial expectation, and his father's fury that clung to the back of his neck like sweat.

Three years later, when my father's work visa ran out and he had to return to the States, his parents offered him his old bedroom, rent-free. Instead, he moved into a high-floor apartment on the Upper East Side of Manhattan, on Seventy-Ninth Street. Gazing out the south-facing windows, he could see Brooklyn far off in the distance, blurry as a greasy postage stamp, its details rubbed away and obscured, the way the world had looked from inside the quiet, sealed cockpit of his plane.

My father returned to Madison Avenue as an advertising copy-
writer and worked his way up to vice president of a major agency. He
ate like a Gentile; he dressed like a Gentile. He filled his closets with
Brooks Brothers sack suits and J. Press shirts monogrammed with
SIA on their cuffs; he carried a small, antique snuff tin; he wore stiff
Lobb's of London wingtips that tore apart his ankles, and whose
soles he had to scuff with a knife, like a little boy's, to keep himself
from slipping. An eligible bachelor straight out of the movie The
Apartment, he decked out his kitchen like a man hell-bent on entertaining: there were silver chafing dishes from Hammacher Schlem-
mer and Arabicaware from Carole Stupell, carbon steel knives from
Hoffritz, and Dansk service for eight from Bloomingdale's. He took
cooking classes with Dione Lucas and learned how to make dishes
that never saw the inside of his parents' kitchen: steak Diane and
duck à l'orange, cherries flambé, and tender, lean silvertip roasts
barded in bacon, specially cut for him at the German butcher
Schaller and Weber. He learned how to bone out and butterfly a pork
loin, open it like a book and stuff it with dried fruit, tie it, and gently
braise it. Every Saturday night, he cooked for the fine-boned, delicate Gentile girls who worked with him at the office, bringing them
back to his apartment after long afternoons spent walking around
the Museum of Modern Art, analyzing the Pollocks and the Fran-
kenthalers, believing secretly that the art possessed no humanity or
warmth. It was just a modernist conceit, he would tell me, an artistic
arrogance, like comparing Bartók to his beloved Chopin: it was rule-
breaking just for the sake of rule-breaking.

"So nu, Mr. Fancy Bachelor—" my grandfather would say during
Shabbos dinner. My father never mentioned girls or had any inclina-
tion to bring one home to meet his parents. He refused to call Mir-
iam Rubenstein, whose mother pleaded with Grandma Bertha to
have Captain America take out her beautiful baby girl. He could find
his own girls to go out with; he would never bring them home to his
parents, though. He would never allow them that close to his life.

"It's bashert, Bertha," Mrs. Rubenstein said to my grandmother.
"The children will be together. I just know it."

It was a fix-up like from the old country; the Hasids still did it. My father refused.

"What's wrong with you anyway? A fagel, maybe?" Grandpa asked, chuckling at the thought that maybe, just maybe, my father liked men.

If you only knew, my father thought.

14

The Fourth Wall

THE WEEKEND BEFORE he moved out of our apartment, my parents and I sat around a square table at the Tung Shing House, draped with a starched, dark gold linen tablecloth. Platters banged in the kitchen and small baskets of beige fried rice noodles with the consistency of baked cardboard appeared in front of us. Tiny dipping plates of duck sauce and incendiary mustard and deep Buffalo china bowls of wonton soup arrived; none of us looked up.

Four nights a week, we ate out: the Tung Shing House; London Lenny's for fried seafood; Cookie's Steakhouse, on the top floor of the Queens Center Mall, where my father ordered chopped steaks passed off as filet mignon, I ate baskets of greasy, deep-fried chicken that shed its salty, dry coating like beach sand from a towel, and my mother pushed around on her plate limpid green iceberg lettuce leaves plucked from the iced Hall crocks at the salad bar; and Jahn's Ice Cream Parlor for foot-long hot dogs. There, ten years earlier, George Hoffmann would perform at my birthday party and turn everything he could lay his hands on into a burst of flame, igniting my lifelong fear of fire.

On this Shabbos night, my parents have decided to punctuate the end of the small life we've made together in Forest Hills over a final Chinese dinner. Three blocks away, at the Forest Hills Jewish Center, services are beginning.

We stare at our empty plates in silence; I am undone by quiet panic that will sit on my shoulder like a parrot for the rest of my life. Cold sweat trickles down between my shoulder blades through the small of my back and into my jeans. My heart races and I try to get up to use the bathroom, but my knees won't hold me up, and I'm certain I'll faint; the wet, cold bathroom floor at the Tung Shing House stinks from ammonia, which will make me sick. I drink tall glasses of ice water as quickly as the waiter can pour them. When they speak, my parents' conversation feels forced, a charade based on the myth of courtliness. I imagine an obituary writer documenting the last moments of our life together, and my parents want to make sure it looks good.

Their end was civil.

At home, there is shouting. Something is flung, a door is slammed.

But tonight, we're at the Tung Shing House, and "Muskrat Love" pours from a small radio in the kitchen. My father chain-smokes Merit filters and stares blankly over my mother's shoulder. Dressed in chocolate brown suede jeans and a tight ribbed, shoulderpadded turtleneck the color of putty, my mother sits next to me, focused on the pork dumplings bobbing like small apples in her bowl. For the first time in years, she actually seems to eat, extracting long slivers of pink-tipped meat from the broth and eating them one by one with her fingers, as though the end of her marriage has suddenly launched a latent appetite. I'm hopeful, suddenly. If she eats, I think, will he stay?

My mother slurps her soup; she pokes and stirs and fishes out of the bowl a flaccid, dark green bok choy leaf. She places the white ceramic spoon in her mouth and makes the queer, contorted face of someone who is politely attempting to extract a chunk of gristle from between two teeth without using her fingers. She dexterously shifts her tongue and I see the muscles in her neck strain and tighten; her

heavily mascaraed eyes scan the dining room for someone's—anyone's—attention: they land on an older man in a powder blue leisure
suit having a quiet dinner with his wife at a table on the other side of
the restaurant. My mother smiles broadly, and I wonder if she knows
him. It's just a game: she has stretched the thick dark green, slippery
bok choy leaf tightly, like a condom, over one of her capped front
teeth.

The man gasps.

"Please, Mrs. Altman," our waiter says, rushing over. "Don't make
fun—please. It's food. You eat it. Please."

"For god's sake—" my father says. His voice shakes with rage. My
face erupts with heat; I can't feel my hands. I've left myself, the way
I left myself when Buck took me hiking in Kissena Park after school,
before my parents came home from work. A slow burn of shame
crawls up into my belly. I gasp with awe at my mother's audacity; she
has broken through the filmy barrier that separates our small family
from the rest of the world. She ropes innocent onlookers into our
story, and then performs for them, the way she did when she was on
television in the 1950s; life is a show, and they watch our story un-
fold the way passersby watch a car crash. The nice man in the leisure
suit gapes at us, his eyes widening with surprise at our story: This
once was a family, well-dressed and mannerly. And then, the mother
smiled.

"Forgive me," she says with dramatic contrition to my father, and
to the man across the room. She places her hand on her chest and
closes her eyes with remorse. She takes another spoonful of soup,
looks for another victim, finds one, and smiles again. They gasp at
her, this bombshell with the blacked-out tooth playacting the ugly
girl her mother assured her she was, many years before. This time,
she has the last laugh.

THE NEXT MORNING, it is the first and last time that the three of us sit
side by side at our Danish modern breakfast counter.

My mother has her usual cigarette and cup of Sanka, and flicks glowing ashes onto her brown earthenware breakfast plate while my father breaks the news to me: she has asked him to leave.

I listen, unmoved and tearless, fixating on a half-eaten box of Entenmann's donuts on the counter that my mother has secretly ravaged during the night. My father sounds far away, like he's making this announcement through one end of a cardboard paper towel tube. I'm already ahead of them: she is a survivor; she will be fine. But I imagine him somewhere on Skid Row chugging Thunderbird from a pint in a brown paper bag, or sleeping fitfully on a stained, blue-ticking mattress at a vermin-infested YMHA, or in the tidy resplendence of one of Aunt Sylvia's four guest rooms. In the piles of diaries I keep from this time—gray cardboard laboratory notebooks covered in Mylar-coated sheets emblazoned with the names of Ivy League colleges I will never attend—the pages that correspond to this sticky, warm day in September are blank.

By 1978, my mother is bringing home a bigger paycheck as a fur model than my father, whose business is failing. She comes home from work later and later every night while my father and I eat frozen dinners in opposite ends of the house; he doesn't have the stomach to cook for the two of us and so he sits at the dining room table, alone, reading the *New York Times*, while I eat in front of the television in my bedroom: there are French bread pizzas heated in the toaster oven that bursts into flame at least once a month; frozen Salisbury steak; frozen Welsh rarebit; sleeves of Mallomars and boxes of Fig Newtons. After dinner, we stand together silently on our terrace, side by side, hanging over the gate eight stories above The Riviera Garden Terrace to see if a taxi or a private car will drop my mother off at The Champs-Élysées Promenade. Sometimes she'll come in at nine, sometimes at eleven, and often after midnight; it's the beginning of the fur season, and she's out with clients and buyers, I hear her tell my father through the bedroom door. This last Saturday morning, she leaves us at the breakfast table, puts on her jacket, and heads into the city for work: it's the time of year when every wealthy woman in New York makes appointments to look at new fur coats. She pats the dog, kisses me on the head, grabs her bag and her keys, and closes the door on her former life as if it were just another day.

THERE IS THE DONUT BOX, and the dog.

There is my father, and his plate of cold bacon and eggs. There he is, standing up, gently placing our plates in the sink.

He opens the hallway closet door, the repository for the family suitcases, and extracts the one they carried on their last trip to Europe. It's beige and soft-sided, stained and covered with peeling travel stickers from France, Austria, and Italy, where my mother sang at Alfredo's on the Piazza Augusto Imperatore in Rome the summer that Aunt Sylvia and Uncle Lee came to visit me at camp. There is the suitcase, unzipped, catching drawerfuls of his life: his underwear and his socks and shirts and a balled-up tangle of striped rep ties from Brooks Brothers. There are brown and gold paisley ascots and identical silk pocket squares, and white vinyl belts that match white loafers. I sit on the bed and watch him. Two weeks later, Uncle Lee rings the doorbell on a weekday morning while I'm still in my robe and, unsmiling, thrusts an envelope into my hands. I'm happy to see him—I'm relieved; he and Aunt Sylvia are so safe, so proper—Hi, Uncle Lee, I chirp like an idiot, while my mother appears in a towel behind me, dripping wet from the shower, and screams for the police. My father can't afford to hire a process server; my uncle, expecting my mother to answer the door, serve the divorce papers to me.

My father's face is red and hot with anguish as he packs; his shoulders rattle like bare bones. He cries out like a broken animal: it's an ancient and preverbal sound and one I don't recognize. After he is gone, Gaga comes over and rifles through our cabinets and the refrigerator. She throws out every edible trace of her former son-in-law and his food: his cans of Spam, his plastic-wrapped packages of Oscar Mayer bacon, his sandwich bags holding the remnants of the fancy hams and charcuterie he liked to bring home from Koch and

Nord, our local German butcher near Forest Hills Gardens. By the time she's finished, all that's left in the cabinets and the fridge are two six-packs of Tab, a container of leftover chow mein from the Tung Shing House, a box of Weaver frozen chicken, and a half-eaten box of Ayds diet candies.

15

Take the Gun; Leave the Tefillin

THE LAST DAYS:

There is the lingering smell of hot, spice-crusted pastrami on thin-sliced rye from Ben's Best deli, a few blocks away from The Marseilles.

There is the tiny black handgun that my father keeps buried under his bar mitzvah tefillin in the top drawer of his highboy dresser.

WHEN I WAS SEVEN and my mother left my father and me alone on a Saturday morning to have her hair done, he took me out for a pastrami sandwich at Ben's, which shared a wall with the Ballet Academy on Queens Boulevard. The Academy was where at age three, I bald-faced lied to my teacher Miss Carolyne and told her at the beginning of class that I'd forgotten to kiss my mother goodbye and needed to find her. Disgusted with being shoe-horned into a pink leotard and ballet slippers—I wanted to be Ken, not Barbie—I packed up my tutu in my patent leather tote bag and found my mother standing outside, having a cigarette in front of Ben's, watching the rotisserie chickens revolve. Each time the door to the deli opened, the smell of pickle brine and schmaltz wafted out and engulfed us. I handed my mother my ballet tote and told her, I quit.

At Ben's, my father ordered pastrami sandwiches for both of us; they arrived unadorned on two small white plates: just seeded bread and dark red meat edged with ripples of lace-white fat. On the table, half-sour pickles floated in a small metal vat, next to a cup of yellow mustard and the can of Cel-Ray soda we shared.

Before that day, I had never eaten pastrami; my mother despised it for being too greasy, and it rarely crossed our threshold unless someone died. The Tung Shing House meant celebration; pastrami meant the end.

Sitting at Ben's with my father and faced with our sandwiches, I was captivated: I loved the smoke and the metallic tinge of the curing salt and the spices. I loved the grease and the fat and the way the blackened ends of the meat, pungent and crisp, were softened by the earthy caraway. I ate quickly, shoving enormous bites of sandwich into my mouth, my eyes closed in animal bliss.

My father and I ate in silence; he seemed preoccupied. When we were done, we left and walked hand-in-hand the three blocks back to The Marseilles.

"There's something I have to show you," my father said to me solemnly when we stood alone in the elevator. Left to our own devices, my father was a different man: quieter, reserved, less quick to anger.

He opened our door and patted the dog on the head, and I followed him past the kitchen and into the bedroom he shared with my mother. He slowly pulled open the top drawer of his tall dresser; I was too small to see into it. He took out his phylactery, last worn by him on the day of his bar mitzvah in 1936, and tossed the jumble of cracked leather straps and dinged wooden blocks onto the bed. Containing sacred Torah scrolls, the phylactery, or tefillin, was traditionally worn as a sign of remembrance that God brought the people Israel out of Egypt and gave them freedom. Buried underneath it was a shiny brown cordovan arm holster; he lifted it out of the drawer and unsnapped the top flap. Inside was a small black handgun with a silver trigger.

"I never want you to touch this," he said. "I want you to know that it's here, but you can't ever touch it. Not without me holding it."

"Is it real?" I whispered, looking up at him.

"It shoots tear gas," he said. He sounded almost apologetic, like he was disappointed in himself for not manning up to a .357.

He let me hold the gun; I cradled it and immediately turned it around and gazed squint-eyed down the barrel. It felt heavy and solid and gorgeously weighted, like the Western-style pearlhandled six-shooter cigarette lighter that Buck kept on his coffee table. When I gave it back to him, my father snapped it into the holster, slipped it over his shoulder, and pulled the belt tight around his rib cage.

We stood side by side and gazed into the mirror: he patted the gun, turned around, and looked over his shoulder, then turned to the side and put his hands on his hips, like a model. He unbuckled the holster and put it back in the drawer, covering it up with the blocks and straps of the tefillin. Every day after that if I was alone in the apartment—even if Gaga was in the kitchen, making dinner—I'd slink into the bedroom, open my father's dresser drawer, shove his tefillin to the side, and take out the pistol, removing the holster and unsnapping the leather flap. I would narrow my eyes and stare down the barrel and wonder whether it was real. The year before he moved out, in 1977, the summer of Sam, my father started wearing his piece when he took the dog out after dinner. I was fourteen, and the idea of my diminutive, horsey, Chopin-loving father packing heat struck me as ridiculous.

"Do you really think that shooting tear gas will protect you?" I asked him one night. I sat on his bed and watched while he slipped his arm through the shoulder holster.

I laughed at him; he slapped me so hard that my jaw rattled. "Do you want a sandwich?" he asked, glaring at me.

An hour later, my father appeared in my bedroom doorway with a brown paper bag splotched with grease, stinking of pastrami brine and a half-sour pickle. The next day, alone in the apartment after school, I went into the bedroom, opened the drawer, took out the gun, and sighted down the barrel in silence.

THAT FALL, the man who owned the pizzeria at the top of The Champs-Élysées Promenade was murdered one night, shot at point-blank range as he walked the half block from the shop home to his apartment in The Marseilles, four flights below ours. For weeks after, we would see his widow—a wan, red-haired woman wearing frosted pink lipstick—floating around our neighborhood in a daze until someone would bring her home. A few weeks later, my father came downstairs one morning to the garage underneath The Riviera Garden Terrace to find a small bullet hole in the driver's side window of his Buick. It went unreported, the mystery unsolved and, until he sold the car a few years later, unmended; my father said it was a constant reminder of the fragility of life.

A few days after he packed up his suitcase and moved back to his mother's house in Brooklyn, my father returned to Forest Hills to remove the other things that were his before he married my mother. He waited in his parked car in the promenade until she left for work, and then he came upstairs to begin the process of parsing the things of his life, while I watched: he packed up his Yma Sumac and Gerry Mulligan records and his teak Garrard stereo, his Hasselblad cameras and his celestial navigation charts, his Yiddish typewriter, his Philip Roth and his Henry Miller. He sent me out to walk the dog, and while I was gone, he quietly slipped their wedding silver set into the carton with his records and put it in the trunk of his car. When I came back upstairs, he was done; the apartment looked vaguely picked-over, as though it had been ravaged by a thief. Then he took me back to Ben's for one last lunch of pastrami sandwiches and half-sour pickles and cans of Cel-Ray soda. Pastrami meant the end, as it always had.

"When will I see you," I said. "I don't know," he said.

He dropped me off and drove away, and I went into what had

been my parents' bedroom. I opened the top drawer of his empty dresser; the pistol was gone. All that was left was his worn tefillin and an ancient dog-eared book of matches from Ben's, stained with a fingerprint of yellow deli mustard.

16

The Mountains

M Y FATHER AND I are sitting side by side at the bar at the massive Sugar Maples Hotel in Maplecrest-in-the-Catskills, a mountain village so small that it's officially called a hamlet. Forty miles south of Albany, down a rural road, it is about as far off the beaten path as a Jewish boy from Brooklyn can get.

There is no borscht in this particular belt, which attracts an almost entirely Irish Catholic and Protestant crowd from the Bronx, Staten Island, and New Jersey. Many of the locals are descendants of Dutch settlers, whose families have been in the area for hundreds of years. Everywhere we look—on T-shirts, coffee mugs, lawn signs, commemorative plaques bolted to buildings, restaurant awnings, hospitals, banks, bridges—is the likeness of Rip Van Winkle, who, according to legend, was plied with moonshine by the ghosts of Henry Hudson's crewmen until he passed out and slept for two decades, waking up to discover that the world had changed around him. There is not a Jew for miles in any direction: there's no Julie Budd singing in the nightclub, no Simon Sez in the lobby, no bottles

of Manischewitz on the dinner table, no card room like the one my
father's mother played pinochle in for thirty summers at The Windsor in South Fallsburg, before it was turned into an ashram. It has
been years since The Sugar Maples' heyday, when whole families
came for eight weeks at a time, and husbands left on Sunday nights
to go back to the city for work, returning the following Friday. The
hotel is a little bit down on its luck, a little bit paint-peeling. Its
clapboard buildings are beginning to sag around the middle, like a
too big mattress on a too small frame; with every passing year, the
buildings fall in on themselves just a little bit more.

I kick the quilted vinyl base of the bar and lean my elbows over
onto its plastic burled walnut top; clamped to an articulated metal
arm attached to the wall near the ceiling is a small hospital television tuned to the 1979 Wimbledon Men's Final. Dusty beams of
summer light shine through the hotel's open french doors; outside
is a paving stone patio decorated with white baskets of bright pink
and purple impatiens. There, in two hours, The Sugar Maples
Hotel will hold its annual July Fourth weekend all-pork barbecue,
after which my father will leave me behind for the whole summer
to work the first unsupervised job I've ever had, as a snack-bar girl.
I will sleep in the employees quarters, in a single room with a corner sink, down the hall from a clean-cut Mormon boy a year away
from going on his mission; a twenty-year-old couple and their six-
year-old daughter, who reeks of the patchouli incense her parents
burn to mask the smell of hash; a bloated blond teenage land-
scaper who puts gin in his bong, and who gets so stoned one night
that he takes a bite out of a lightbulb, mistaking it for an ice cream
cone.

"Gibson?" Jack Doherty, the ginger-haired bartender, asks my father, wiping down the bar top with a terrycloth rag. My father nods
his head and stubs out a cigarette in a square hotel ashtray, and immediately lights another.

"And you?" Jack asks me. I am sixteen. I rub my neck; I don't
answer.

"Give her a Genny Cream," my father says, "in a Collins glass."

He has always allowed me small amounts of alcohol from as far back as I can remember; it's a strongly held cultural belief that giving young children alcohol in restricted quantities on a regular basis will mitigate curiosity and curb addiction. As a child, I drink tiny glasses of Manischewitz at Passover, spoonfuls of Slivovitz in the winter, thimbles of Harveys Bristol Cream at Thanksgiving, and shot glasses of Bordeaux at the secret, fancy lunches my father and I have in Manhattan while my mother is out having her hair done. At three years old and in love with the metallic tang of bitterness on my tongue, my parents and I are on our way home from a family outing and I wail and scream like a siren until my father stops the car some-place off the New Jersey Turnpike and buys a six-pack of Schlitz. He pops open a can, gives me a few sips, and throws out the rest. Sated, I sleep in the backseat of his Barracuda until we reach Forest Hills, and my father has to carry me into our apartment in a pink party dress and white patent leather Mary Janes, a damp cloud of hops and yeast swirling around my lips.

But until now, I have never sat at a bar next to him and had a drink that's been ordered specifically for me.

"Jewish girls don't sit at bars," my mother said one night at Max-well's Plum in Manhattan, a few months earlier. I'd climbed onto the barstool while we waited for Ben, her furrier boyfriend, to join us for dinner. The bartender, in a tight black T-shirt, looked at me smugly, leaning over my head to pass off a white wine spritzer to a bearded, open-shirted man behind me, a gold ankh around his neck.

"Get down!" she shouted through lacquered fuchsia lips while Gloria Gaynor's divorce anthem, I Will Survive, blasted from a mas-sive speaker hanging above the bar.

I hopped off the stool and stood lip-glossed and sullen next to her, sweating in the block-shouldered, sheared champagne beaver jacket she borrowed from the showroom, as though putting me in a fur might suddenly compel me towards feminine coyness. I felt like I was in drag.

On this lovely summer afternoon in upstate New York, Jack Doherty carefully places a gin Gibson in a glass the size of a fishbowl—one onion, no twist—in front of my father, followed by a tall Genesee Cream Ale topped off with a thick head of stocking-colored froth in front of me.

"Like love in a canoe . . ." my father says in his best fake radio announcer voice as I lift my glass to take a sip. He elbows me gently in the ribs and winks: this is my punch line cue, his call to my response.

". . . fucking close to water," I answer, winking back, unsmiling. I roll my eyes and squirm on my barstool, hold my glass up, and my father carefully taps it with his Gibson, which spills a little of the clear liquid over the rim.

"Cheers," we say together, like old Navy buddies.

We are a divorced father and his spotty, panic-prone teenage daughter who he is about to leave for an entire summer in a lush Christian upstate New York mountain town where she is the token Jew, and where Gaga has warned her that they may or may not look for her horns; where she will be paid minimum wage to make eight weeks of cheap ham and mayo sandwiches on white bread for cigar-smoking shuffleboard players in wife beaters and kind Italian grandmothers who wear their flowered bathing caps all day and who, more than once, will press rosary beads into her hand after she feeds them, slicing their sandwiches in half on a precise angle, tossing their iceberg lettuce with just the right amount of Wish-Bone Italian salad dressing, and slipping them a cookie and a small cup of coffee at the end of their meal; where, during the employee parties that take place every night, she will learn to ingest vast, almost inhuman quantities of liquor—a screw-top jug of Almaden Mountain Rhine passed around a circle of off-duty employees by thumb-hook, vodka injected into a watermelon with a hypodermic begged from the hotel nurse, grain alcohol spiked with cherry-flavored Hi-C out of a galvanized trough—with the sole, resolute purpose of getting completely and utterly tanked as quickly as possible.

Jack Doherty laughs out loud, and shakes his head.

"A regular Shecky Greene she is," he says, nodding over to me. "When are you sending her out on the road?"

This has become our shtick since he's moved out. It's as though his switch has been flipped: my father is no longer a hot wire ready to burst into flame, warm and charming one minute and unpredictably enraged the next. My father-without-my-mother has become a wholly different animal, as though he's stepped into a phone booth like Clark Kent becoming Superman; all signs of his temper have melted away like snow in a rainstorm, replaced by a soft, mildly ribald sense of humor as pliable as Silly Putty. He comments on the absurd in everything and teaches me the punch lines to the jokes—some tired and worn; some so lewd that the listeners laugh and cringe at the same time while they watch me speak mechanically, like my father's Charlie McCarthy—that he's been telling for half a century, hauling them out whenever we're together. In Maplecrest, he wants the locals to love us like we're court jesters. Hotel employees and guests flock to him wherever he appears: in the dark, wood-paneled lobby, on the tennis court, in the cavernous dining room that seats seven hundred, in the bar. Wherever he is, there is a joke, and barks of laughter: an overweight guest looks from behind like two bulldogs fighting under a blanket. His guest room is so small that the mice are hunchback. The new snack-bar girl, Emma, who, according to hotel gossip, fucks her way through every week's new guest roster, spends so much time on her back, you could sell ad space on the soles of her feet. And the Genny Cream Ale is so thin and wan that it's like love in a canoe: fucking close to water. My father, whose Coney Island nightstand creaks under the weight of Lion Feuchtwanger and Bernard Malamud and John Cheever, has turned before my eyes into Don Rickles.

But his laughter is bottomless; it invariably erupts into an explosion of uncontrollable coughing, which devolves into a fountain of tears that he can't stop. This is his B-side: he is a Jewish night fighter pilot, an advertising executive in a Brooks Brothers sack suit, the little brother of Aunt Sylvia, whose carefully constructed world is the picture of social perfection and safety, which he will never attain. He is a newly divorced man looking for a toehold as though life itself is the smooth face of a mountain and he, a climber looking for a place to hang on and perch. He gravitates to places where no one knows him, where he—where we both—can start fresh: new lives.

We sit together at The Sugar Maples bar, side by side, and like Rip Van Winkle, we drink the numbing nectar of somnambulance and wait, anxiously, for the world to change around us, to accept us, to approve.

MY FATHER AND I SPEND every weekend together: he arrives in Forest Hills on Friday afternoon, parking his car in my high school rotunda and waving me over with a cold bottle of cola he has waiting on the passenger side floor. He lets the motor idle; my classmates and I pour out of the building and into the street, and while they pair up and head out to a nearby pizzeria for a snack, I spy my father's car; I get in, we drive away. We have late lunches and early dinners at restaurants my mother would never dare set foot in, which my father fetishizes as being real, authentic New York: The Belmore Cafeteria, which smells like puke and Lysol, and where my new Bass Weejuns stick to the floor, and the chocolate brown gravy on the spongy gray meatloaf comes out of an industrial food service can. We go to The Automat, where we open small plastic doors to retrieve our food: rubbery orange cheese sandwiches on white bread, and cold blueberry pie on a thick, pasty crust that attaches itself to the roof of my mouth like dental putty. We sit at the counter next to off-duty cops at Brennan and Carr, and gorge ourselves on warm roast beef sandwiches drenched in jus that dribbles down my chin and onto the pressed Brooks Brothers oxford cloth shirts and khakis that my father has taken to outfitting me in since the divorce.

Gone are my stiff Wranglers, my rodeo belts, my fringed jackets, my pearl-snap gingham yoked shirts, and my Dingo boots: my father has assembled a new wardrobe for me—a new persona—that exudes conventionality and traditionalism and old WASP wealth and security. It's a carapace of safety, a way to fend off the bedlam that we have both grown up with, and I crave it the way an alcoholic craves a scotch; I slip into this Presbyterian facade like a hand into a velvet glove. Conformity will allow me to leave the past behind, he believes, and propel me into a different, more predictable kind of world, where children aren't beaten or preyed upon, and life itself is orderly and fair. There are monogrammed Shetland sweaters in murky Scottish colors of pine and heather; wide wale corduroys in emerald greens and Pepto-Bismol pinks; high-necked Carroll Reed turtlenecks emblazoned with ducks and lobsters, which my father buys for me by the dozen. There's an Irish fisherman sweater that smells of sheep lanolin and salt, and is so thick that when I wear it, I can't bend my arms; a navy blue Brooks Brothers blazer purchased for me in the boy's department, where he believes the clothes are better made; there are square-toed Docksides, round-toed Top-Siders, shin-high L.L. Bean duck boots, and low rubber moccasins and lace-up brown Bluchers and band-sleeved Lacostes in every shade and a wool plaid-lined hunting coat the color of burning sugar, which has an interior pocket the width of my back, to carry home dead ducks from my hunting party. For Thanksgiving at Aunt Sylvia's house, the first since the divorce, he buys me a special outfit: a black cashmere turtleneck and floor-length Black Watch kilt held closed with a safety pin the size of a harpoon; I carry a dark gray, wooden-handled Bermuda bag containing a linen hanky and a tube of ChapStick. I comb my thick, frizzy, shoulder-length hair back, attach a green and white grosgrain band to my head like a clamp, and spray it in place with Aqua Net; it's so tight that I spend the evening looking surprised.

"You look gorgeous," my father says, as I crawl into his car when he picks me up on The Champs-Élysées Promenade; my mother has already left to celebrate Thanksgiving with Ben's friends in a loft downtown.

At dinner, I clasp my hands tightly at the table, which is gleaming with my aunt's Greek Key silver. We pass her our plates; Uncle Lee, his tie tucked into his shirt, carves the turkey with the precision of a surgeon. My cousins' conversations weave back and forth and over and around each other like a loom; in a moment of silence, Aunt Sylvia turns to me.

"We are so glad that you are here," she says, unsmiling. "Tell me; how are your boyfriends?"

I get home that night and my mother is sitting in her robe on the living room love seat with the dog, reading Cosmopolitan.

"How was Thanksgiving?" I ask, putting my bag down. "You look like an old woman—like Dame May Whitty, walking on the moors," she answers. "Come give me a kiss." She holds her arms up; an invitation.

OUR WEEKENDS ARE RULED by food and eating: there are greasy spoons in Hell's Kitchen and German biergartens in Queens and the Brasserie in midtown Manhattan, where we sit at the immense horseshoe-shaped counter and the gruyère melts and drips down the sides of the onion soup crocks and hardens like cement. We go downtown dressed in wool flannels and cashmere, and my father parks his new car—a silver GMC lowrider sports car with a black racing stripe down the hood—on Barrow Street, and we walk north, towards Fourth Street, and past the Cubbyhole, where shorthaired women are outside in a throng, waiting to get in; they look at us and I glance away quickly, across the street, at my feet, at anything but them. We walk over to Bleecker Street together, my arm snaked through his; he positions me on the inside, away from the curb, because, he says, the man should always be closest to the street in case a passing car splashes puddle water up and onto the curb. We walk to the Five Oaks, where every other couple in the room is comprised of two men in snug polo shirts and low-slung, tight jeans, their hair shorn close and their beards shaved down, and the energy of the room is a throbbing knot of hormones and flirting and snark. Manhattan's trendiest new dish is on every table: salmon and vegetables encased in a pinch-sealed envelope of foil that is baked and slit open at the table, where it releases a cloud of steam and herbs and sea. At Randazzo's Clam Bar in Sheepshead Bay, we eat massive trays of shrimp and lobster fra diavolo with platters of spaghetti in white

clam sauce, seeded yellow semolina loaves, and carafes of cheap
Chianti. They bring one small water glass for my father; he asks for
a second one for me, and we sip the wine together until the din in
the cavernous space softens and clouds like I've got my head under
a pillow and my ears begin to ring.

It's at Randazzo's one Friday night that I get up to use the ladies'
room; a wave of chilly queasiness passes through my chest and I
stand and the floor tilts under my feet like an amusement park ride;
I make it to the bathroom, holding the backs of the dining room's
chairs and pulling myself forward, hand over hand, like a Marine on
an obstacle course, until I push open the ladies' room door, pull at
the monogrammed collar of my white turtleneck, and pass out slowly,
slithering down to the tile floor.

"You all right," I hear in a hard Brooklyn accent, and I am propped
up against the bathroom wall by a gum-smacking girl in a satin baseball jacket and high tops, who hauls me up by my armpits and
splashes water on my face. I've spiked a 105-degree fever exactly
seven hours after eating a sour tuna sandwich at the greasy spoon
across the street from my father's Manhattan office; it's crept up on
me slowly, like a pickpocket, and then, defenses down, attacked.
That weekend, while my mother and Ben escape the city for his
country club in Armonk, I lie shaking on my late Grandpa Henry's
horsehair mattress in Coney Island while my father sleeps on the
sofa in the living room. The pain is relentless; I feel as though I'm
being repeatedly skewered by half a dozen dull bread knives, and it
makes me want to die. For seventy-two hours, I hallucinate in vivid
and gorgeous detail; my cousin Maya the ballerina, dead before I
was born, the family myth—she had been so beautiful and so kind,
everyone said—lifts the hem of her white ballet skirt and steps out,
first one foot and then the other, of the gilt-edged frame that hangs
on the narrow wall between the two bedroom closets where she has
been living on poster board. She floats around my grandfather's bed
in a crinkling cloud of voile and lace before gathering up her skirts
and climbing back inside the frame; she turns and waves at me over
her shoulder, her black-lined Cleopatra eyes blinking slowly. I hold

my hand up to wave, and her long dark hair, stuffed into a ballerina's chignon, becomes a soft aureole of black filament swirling around what is now an older, unsmiling face staring back at me, and I smell Jean Naté and turkey gravy and it's Aunt Sylvia. I snap back to consciousness, and Brooklyn, and my father is sitting by my bedside, staying there all weekend with a cool dishrag on my head, like a handkerchief on a lampshade. Every time I wake up, I'm wearing different pajamas; I've soaked through them all—first my own, and then my grandmother's from the 1940s, and then my father's starched, button-down Brooks Brothers shirts. I've been washed down with rubbing alcohol and changed repeatedly, like a baby; I'm grateful that he's there, and sickened that he's seen my teenage body, and I pass out again into a haze of blackness. Each time I open my eyes, we gape and stare at each other through the murk of obligation and regret; the fever has muddled my brain, like I'm in twilight sleep.

"I'm sorry," he says, the morning my fever begins to break. "Don't," I say. I tell him I'm exhausted, that everything is foggy, that I can't think straight, that I need to sleep.

"But I want you to know," he says. His face is red and beginning to twist.

"I can't absolve you," I say. "Do you love me?" he says. "Daddy, I'm here, aren't I?"

I will never know if what we say is real or imagined.

WHEN THE WEATHER TURNS WARM, we become regular weekend guests at Sugar Maples; my father handles the advertising for the family who owns the place, which includes white and green clapboard residential buildings, the lobby, the bar, tennis courts, shuffleboard, basketball, an archery range, softball fields, and hiking trials. The hotel's cavernous, free-standing dining room is flanked on both sides by two tiny churches, which restrict alcohol from being served on the property anywhere but in the bar. There is no wine with dinner, no martinis on the patio behind the main building, no cold beers during the annual employee-guest softball game.

At sixteen, I'm too old to attend camp and too young to be a counselor, and my mother is spending every weekend at Ben's country club. My father has called the hotel owner and gotten me a job in the snack bar, until school starts in September and I have to return home. For the next two months, I am paid minimum wage, room and board included, and given one day off per week. I sleep on an old, lumpy striped mattress covered in starched sheets that stink of bleach and feel like sandpaper, in a single room upstairs from the lobby. I eat in the employee dining room—the EDR—three times a day, family-style. On my days off, I tag along with the older employees who have cars—olive green Plymouth Dusters and rusting-paneled Country Squire wagons into which we illegally pile nine—with glove compartments packed with rolling papers and roach clips, and sticky half-empty pints of Southern Comfort and blackberry brandy. Sometimes we go to Woodstock and sometimes to Lenox; sometimes, when the weather is hot, we go to the Esopus Creek in nearby Phoenicia, where we tube languidly down the river for hours, stripping off our wet cutoff shorts and T-shirts and bake our naked, glandular selves dry on the massive, flat rocks that dot the bank.

I don't know these people, but the body armor I have worn like a shell dissolves around them like sugar in water. Safety, when she arrives, feels loving and kind; I don't recognize her, even as she wraps herself around me like a swaddling blanket.

All summer, I will never think of home, except for Gaga, who I call every few days from an office rotary phone. The village operator patches me through to Forest Hills, free of charge, like I'm phoning from Mayberry. If I listen closely, I can hear the Long Island Rail Road rumble behind Gaga's voice, which I miss so much that I actually gasp.

17

Cooking

URING THE SCHOOL YEAR, she makes potato latkes and diaphanous matzo meal pancakes the size of saucers. She makes salty matzo brei egg scrambles with caramelized onion and a shower of black pepper. There are kugels sweet and savory, roast chickens kneaded with vegetable oil and paprika, their metal kosher certification tags dangling from their ankle cartilage like charms from a bracelet. There is stuffed breast of veal sewn up with a carpet needle she bought special from a flooring store on Queens Boulevard, and in the heat, chef salads into which she slices neat triangles of cold cuts: long sheets of Swiss cheese differentiated from American only by virtue of color and hole; bologna; Hebrew National salami; Oscar Mayer boiled ham. There are television snacks of saltines and spray cheese; grilled cheese and bacon at McCrory's on Sixty-Third Drive served to me by a strawberry blond shiksa wearing a peach-toned, triple-weave polyester apron who she introduces to me as "my lady friend." There are frozen fish sticks cooked in a smoking toaster oven that always catches fire; doughy french bread pepperoni pizzas;

Weaver fried chicken drumsticks; Swanson's Hungry-Man dinners; blueberry blintzes topped with dollops of sour cream; cold leftover brisket stuffed into soft onion pockets; chopped chicken livers on Russian black bread so dense and dark that it looks like a starless midnight sky.

What shall I make for your return? she writes to me in her letters, when I'm at sleepaway camp and, then, working at the hotel. The question feels formal, asked in the old-fashioned style of a mother writing to her son off fighting at Gettysburg or the Somme. What would you like me to have waiting for you? she says, and I believe at that moment my universe is comprised of just the two of us: Gaga, whose daughter's attention has turned towards a new life as a single woman in late 1970s Manhattan, and me, whose world is stitched together by her grandmother—the foul-tempered, unsmiling woman who once loved another woman. After the divorce, Gaga and I spend our days together quietly at the kitchen table while my mother is out with Ben, and my father is living in Brooklyn with his mother who, after sixty years, is still trying to feed him the borscht that he has hated since he was a baby. He rails and fights with her as though nothing has changed for them; nothing has.

Gaga and I are heretics, watchers, quick to temper, brokenhearted. Our lives begin and end in the kitchen, connected to each other by love and the fraying cords of domestic madness and disappointment: I am my mother's daughter. My mother is Gaga's daughter. Together, we form a triangulation of anger and disappointment that dissipates only when Gaga and I are alone together. She is my safety net and my world, even with her temper that leaves our apartment door slammed, our drinking glasses broken, my sneakers—when I choose to spend Saturday nights with my father rather than with her after the divorce—once spat upon in a torrent of fury that we both choose, somehow, to forget. What shall I make for your return? she asks, and I live for this question as much for the food as for the love, because the food is the love. I dream of her goulash—a mosaic of sinewy, kosher chuck roast that she cubes by holding large pieces of the meat in her left hand and slicing it with a cheap flexible serrated steak knife held in her right like she's sectioning an apple. More than once she nicks herself, dropping tiny beads of scarlet blood along with the cubes into her lime green plastic mixing bowl. There is a long massage with ancient paprika and the addition of slivered onions and smashed garlic cloves, half a can of Del Monte tomato sauce, and then the dump into a squat, avocado-colored Teflon pot into which she slices unpeeled nuggets of floury potato to thicken the contents into the consistency of slow, meaty sludge. What shall I make for your return? she asks me in a letter, and I write back and say, Goulash, even in the heat of the late summer, and she writes back and says, All right, my darling, I'll make it for you.

"She never called me 'darling,'" my mother snarls in the car on the way home from meeting the camp bus with my father. She folds down the makeup mirror and glares at me sitting in the backseat while I read Gaga's letters, which I carry in my knapsack, aloud. I never read them out loud again.

Gaga doesn't come with my parents to pick me up from the camp bus. A year later, after the divorce, she won't meet my father's car downstairs at it pulls into The Champs-Élysées Promenade after the long drive home from Sugar Maples. Instead, I find her upstairs at our white Chambers stove, stirring her pot in silence, droplets of sweat dripping down her lined forehead. She folds and turns and mixes and blends and after an unfathomable, shocking hug when I burst through the door—she isn't a hugger—I sit down at the breakfast counter in our narrow galley kitchen with my mother's mostly forgotten, half-empty boxes of Ayds diet candies in front of me, and Gaga reaches over my shoulder and puts down a small melamine bowl and a spoon and I eat in silence with her standing over my shoulder, clacking her false teeth together to keep them from slipping, and my heart bursts open.

There is goulash on toast; goulash on spaetzle; goulash on rice; goulash on challah. There is leftover goulash—goulash that I eat alone in the early morning hours before my mother returns from an evening out with Ben, goulash at midnight, goulash at four in the morning when I wake up and can't sleep. The pot, its contents slowly receding like the ocean, takes up the entire bottom shelf in our fridge, but I never think to decant it into a smaller container. When the silver slashes of the dinged Teflon begin to peek through, I ration the stew, pulling the shards and shreds of meat into strings, adding meager tablespoons of hard New York City tap water to the leftovers in order to lengthen the sauce, and her love. When the pot is nearly empty, its sides and bottom lacquered with the remnants of meat juice and tomato and dried white potato starch, I heat it up to melt them into a final puddle the size of the half dollars I collect, and I use a small piece of stale challah to sponge down the sides and the corners of the pot, like its content was pure gold.

What shall I make for your return? Gaga asks in her letters. Goulash—the food her Hungarian immigrant mother made her—ties us together, grandmother to granddaughter, outlier to outlier.

Make me your heart, I think, and she does.

SHE WAS BORN WITH A mean mouth," my mother says about Gaga.

"What's that?" I ask when I'm a young teenager. "I don't know," she says. "But just look at her."

Instead of a downturn of sad resignation, Gaga's mouth is pulled taut as a wire, rarely smiling or moving. I have a cousin with a mouth curled into a perpetual snarl like a mountain lion. Mine is crooked and unsure, like my father's and his father's. But Gaga's is a tight red line, a boundary so straight that I expect it to creak like an old floorboard when she opens it to speak or to fight with anyone who dares cross her: the grocery store delivery boy, who she accuses of short-changing her; the sixth grade teacher who bullies and torments me in front of a classroom of laughing schoolmates; my mother, when she stays overnight at Ben's and skulks back into our apartment just before sunrise.

Gaga came into the world in 1901 on the precipice of a new century, almost a year to the day after Queen Victoria's death: she inherits her mother's love of music and her father's ferocious disposition. A massive, barrel-chested six-foot-four Budapest-born Hungarian hussar turned kosher butcher who wrings the scrawny necks of kosher chickens in the feather-covered back room of his Williamsburg store, he sets six-year-old Gaga on a ladder over an immense cauldron of boiling water and instructs her to submerge the dead birds by their feet, to loosen their feathers. I imagine her holding the creatures, the hot water splattering up onto the dress that her mother, Esther, has sewn for her; she accidentally drops one whole chicken into the water—it slips out of her sweaty baby hands—and her father chases her around the store, taking off a blood-splattered boot and throwing it at his oldest child until she runs out the door and down Broadway, tears of frustration caught in her throat. Every afternoon, she tries to fix her mistake, and to please him, to make things right; she spends her days after school singing to herself while sitting outside the store on an upturned wooden crate, plucking feathers from piles of birds, ankle-deep in viscera and plumage, directly across the street from what will become, a century later, Marlow & Daughters, the greatest pork emporium in New York.

Gaga is the oldest of six—five girls and a boy, Herman, who will die during the 1918 flu epidemic—and their mother, Esther, a tiny, smallpox-scarred homemaker with a sweet soprano voice turned her brownstone into a boardinghouse after her husband died at forty-two. The only way she can keep the family together and keep the roof over her children's heads is to house and feed perfect strangers for five dollars a week. Day and night, while World War I rages on the other side of the Atlantic, Esther stands in her kitchen cooking for her family and the German and Austrian and Irish and Italian and Polish boarders who sleep and bathe and eat side by side with her Jewish children, coddling and loving them, and teaching them the languages of their homelands just so that they can hear them spoken by innocent voices: by the time Gaga marries Grandpa Philip in 1934, she is fluent in German and speaks Italian as if she herself came directly off the boat from Palermo.

There is a dusty, dog-eared photograph of Esther that I am shown over and over again, and this is how I imagine her whenever I imagine her: her thinning, graying hair pulled back in a loose bun, smudged round Emma Goldman glasses perched on the end of her nose, black bump-toe shoes, and an apron covering a thin cotton dress laden with petunias. Every day, before the boarders come home, she takes an afternoon break and ushers Gaga and her sisters into the parlor and teaches them how to sing "And the Band Played On" in harmony around the massive upright Kranich & Bach piano that stands in the middle of the room.

"She was always working," Gaga told me when I was older, "always working. Always in the kitchen; always feeding people, whoever came by." When one overnight visitor, an opera singer who was performing that night in Manhattan, gave an impromptu recital in the parlor for the other boarders, the man's manager, Gatti-Cazza, found Esther sitting on a stool in the kitchen, taking a break from her day's work, a damp dishcloth in her hands, her head resting against the doorjamb and listening to the overnight guest sing Puccini.

"Take your apron off, Mrs. Gross, and please come into the parlor—" Gatti-Cazza said, holding his hand out. She took it and followed him into the long, cavernous room, and quietly sat out of view while Enrico Caruso sang Vecchia Zimarra. Gaga said that her mother hummed it sweetly to herself for the rest of her life, even when the asthma was killing her, when she could barely breathe and they had to bring an oxygen tank into the apartment she shared with my mother, Gaga, and Grandpa Philip, thirty years later.

"A RELIGION; it was like her religion," Gaga would say while she cooked for me, telling me this story of her mother, Esther, who died in 1948, and who made it her life's work to feed and provide nourishment and sustenance to perfect strangers, even as the only worlds they knew, thousands of miles away, were imploding.

"Maybe because," Gaga says. She speaks through lips as taut as a cord, putting a bowl of goulash down in front of me one day after school. Chronically soaked with perspiration, even in the dead of winter, Gaga wipes her eyes with a greasy, flowered terrycloth dishtowel and goes back into the kitchen.

"But why," I ask her. "Why would she want to feed people she didn't even know?"

I have been taught over the years, by Aunt Sylvia, by my mother, that cooking for other people is labor, that it's nothing to be proud of or ever to aspire to; the act of providing sustenance is something to be embarrassed by, the downstairs to our upstairs. The need—the desire—for sustenance and nurturing is even worse: it's shameful.

After my family has fallen apart, after my father has left and moved back to Brooklyn and my mother is out every night, the only thing I want or need is Gaga, just the two of us, alone together, sometimes listening to music, sometimes not. She tells me the story of her mother, Esther, and the boardinghouse, and the time that Caruso came to stay and sang Puccini, and she feeds my heart and soul, plate after plate, bowl after bowl. When she is in it, the kitchen is my safe room, the place where I am most secure, protected, sustained.

"Do you know that you were named for her?" she repeats, and I say, "Yes, I do."

"What shall I make for you, Elissala?" Gaga says to me every day, and she stands in the kitchen, and she cooks for me.

YEARS LATER, after I leave for college in Boston, after my mother marries Ben and moves into Manhattan, Gaga will step out of the building she moved my mother to in 1960, leaving Grandpa Philip to sleep alone in his furniture store in Williamsburg with nothing but Sister Redempta and his homing pigeons for company; Gaga will stand in the middle of The Champs-Élysées Promenade and look up at our apartment in The Marseilles, occupied, after eighteen years, by strangers.

"No one left to cook for," she says, when she calls me in my dormitory room in Boston. "No one left to eat with. When are you coming home?"

Six months later, at five in the morning, Ben will call my dorm room: "Gaga is gone," he tells me. A massive heart attack in the middle of the night.

"Don't come—don't even try to get home," he says as I stand at the window facing west over Commonwealth Avenue. Enormous snowflakes the size of half dollars flutter past me; the wind blows them up and sideways and down; I can't focus on them. Ben's voice is distant, as if he's calling me from another place and time, and I can barely hear him. On that morning, an early April nor'easter—a freak springtime snowstorm—will blanket and shut down the entire East Coast within hours. The trains will stop running and the airports will shut down and the roads will be abandoned. I will never have the chance to say goodbye.

18

Family

THE EMPLOYEE DINING ROOM—the EDR—at Sugar Maples is long and narrow, like a white clapboard single-wide set upon a cement foundation. It's tucked behind the dining room, between the massive metal walk-in refrigerator that's the size of my bedroom in Forest Hills, and the hotel laundry, with its humming industrial front-loading washers and dryers emitting hot chemical vapors morning and night. When the wind is right, and even when it's not, the stench of souring, cheesy milk spills out through the walk-in's rotting rubber door gaskets, which are disintegrating with age. The peeling EDR doors—wood-framed, double-screened from top to bottom, torn in spots, the desiccated carcasses of ancient flies trapped and rattling between them—swing open and closed all day, with employees going in and out for free cups of industrial coffee that tastes like I've been sucking on a metal pipe.

We range in age from sixteen to thirty-one, and we gather at the EDR three times a day; a green plastic transistor radio sits on the windowsill, blaring an endless loop of America and The Allman

Brothers and Pure Prairie League. The groundskeepers—we call them the Yardbirds—come in for breakfast first, because they've been doing manual labor since before dawn and are starving. Jim, a guitar-playing redhead with a frizzy short ponytail held in place by a blue bandana, wears round John Lennon glasses and a friendly, dimpled smile. He cups his hands around a chipped Buffalo china mug of weak coffee softened with curdling fake creamer, and sits down at the head of the thirty-foot-long table. Psychopathic Bill—Psycho Bill for short, since the night he took a bite out of a lightbulb—who works in the laundry, is blond, ruddy, and perpetually toasted; for no reason, he flings a plate of powdered scrambled eggs and undercooked, fatty bacon overhand like a Frisbee at gorgeous, leggy Jennifer, who sips her coffee like she's enjoying tea at the Ritz. She is one of three prim, Lilly Pulitzer–clad sorority girls who have come up from New Orleans to work as guest liaisons, and who will not survive the summer. Eric, the nephew of a well-known NFL running back, lives in town and is the only black kid in the entire county; shy, softspoken, and so handsome that people gasp when they see him, he makes a breakfast plate for himself—eggs, bacon, toast, sausage of unknown provenance—and sits down directly across from me, looking up every few minutes to smile.

Emma, who works with me in the snack shack, is from Shaker Heights and attends Exeter. Sixteen, anorexic, dressed in three-sizes-too-big white Smith overalls over a tight tank top revealing a thatch of mahogany fur nestled in the crook of each armpit, her masses of long brown hair stuffed into a tweed newsboy cap like magic snakes into a trick beer can, she plants herself next to me as I drink my first cup of sweet, black coffee. She scoots over close, in a cloud of sweat and patchouli; she links arms with me while I try to eat, and her touch sends a shock wave of electricity through my body and into my hand that nearly makes me drop the piece of incinerated toast I'm chewing on. She gives me an affectionate peck on the cheek and touches the small of my back, and my heart cracks open like an uncooked egg.

I feel mild numbness when I break two fingers on Camp Towanda's field hockey pitch and when I blow out my knee on an icy Vermont ski slope. I feel a leaden deadness at my core when Buck slips me away to the verdant depths of Kissena Park among the mugwort and the bittersweet, on the days he's supposed to be tutoring me in math, or when my father issues a brief, violent beating in the basement of the Tung Shing House, outside the ladies' room. But on this morning, with Emma's hand on my back and the clang of used plates dropping into the rubber washtub in the kitchen, my stomach turns over and every cell in my body pulses with an unknowable, alien electricity that leaves the taste of shame in my mouth, like bile. Tears burn my eyes; I suck down my coffee to hold them off.

"G'morning, babycakes," Steve bends down and whispers in my other ear, stretching his long legs beneath the table. He is a beanpole, with straight, sun-dappled hair the color of straw and bright cornflower blue eyes. This morning, he's made two plates for himself, piled high with eggs, bacon, slices of buttered, immolated toast, and fried potatoes; he balances it all plus two glasses of whole milk plus a can of warm Coke that he's liberated from the bar near the lobby. Steve works wherever he's needed at the hotel: as a stand-in waiter in the dining hall, a painter, a mechanic, a camp counselor for the young children of guests, an archery instructor who will, on a dare, shoot out the tires on the hotel laundry truck, a busboy, a mail sorter, a housekeeper, a line cook, a dishwasher. He's in perpetual, constant motion; he's loud and brash and hilarious, and he doesn't give a shit. I'm the new girl, the one in the Lacoste shirts and the leather Tretorns, a conquest he'll never have to see again after the summer; Steve follows me around like a stray dog. And so does Emma, who floats from guys, including Steve, to girls, and back again, with all the fluidity of a river. I'm unaccustomed to the attention, which makes me feel naked; for the very first time in my life, I relish it.

Jim the Yardbird drains his coffee cup, gets up to leave, and playfully ruffles my hair as he walks past me.

"Have a good day, kiddos," he says. I look up at him standing behind me, and I smile.

"So what's happening today?" Steve asks, shoveling eggs into his mouth by the soup spoonful.

"The snack shack from nine to five," I say. "And my father is coming up. It's Friday."

"So does this mean I can come by for an afternoon snack before Daddy arrives?" He puckers his lips and squinches his eyes tight.

"For God's sake, you are so completely gross," Emma says.

She pulls her hat off and whacks him over the head. He swoons and bats his eyelashes at her.

"You love me, em—admit it." "Shut up, Steve—I do not."

"Do too," he answers, puckering up, this time at Emma, who stands up and storms out of the EDR, slamming the screen door behind her.

There is no camp counselor, no manager, no parent, no boss, no babysitter, no caregiver, no person of authority to stop the banter and the food fights and the teasing.

When I call home, my mother doesn't ask me if I'm having a good time, or what the weather is like, or what I'm eating.

"Do they know you're Jewish?" she wants to know, and I don't—I can't—answer. Whoever or whatever I am, for the first time in my life, appears to make no difference. At Sugar Maples, we work together, we talk together, we eat together, we fight together, we get drunk together, we smoke pot together, we nap together like a pile of puppies in the employee living quarters just above the lobby. Open any door during any break, and there, passed out across a bed, will be two, three, four of us, sleeping like exhausted toddlers. By summer's end, I will lose my virginity on the linoleum backroom floor of the snack shack during a mountain rainstorm to a blond, lanky boy in a Keep On Truckin' T-shirt, with Amie, what you wanna do thrumming in the background. Steve is kind and clumsy and mostly gentle, fumbling with the single, lone Trojan that his Marine brother gave him, and that he's been carrying around in his wallet all summer. It happens quickly, we both dream of Emma.

. . .

THERE ARE A FEW DATES: one-offs with attractive women, all lanky and svelte like my mother, all of them Gentile, as though my father is taunting Grandpa Henry all the way to the grave. There is Betsy McDouglass, a dark-haired commercial accountant from Albuquerque, who came to New York once a month to see clients. Grace Falk, a black leather–jacketed museum administrator, drags my father, dressed in his Brooks Brothers costume, to hear Lou Reed and John Cale at The Kitchen. He vows to never see her again, except the sex is so good.

"Shit, Dad, I don't need to hear this," I groan.

We are eating racks of marinated, dripping baby back ribs at O'Lunney's, a sticky-floored Irish bar in midtown Manhattan, where we've gone to hear Country Gazette. My friends are listening to Blondie and The Clash and Cheap Trick, and I'm in love with Christian bluegrass, and the band sings Louvin Brothers songs about Jesus and redemption and faith.

"Well, who else am I going to tell it to? Your grandmother?" He pours himself, and then me, a beer from a scuffed plastic pitcher that has just landed on our table.

"You're going to have to find someone else to talk to," I say, "because I can't—"

"But aren't you happy for me?" he shouts over the mandolin solo. He looks desperate and red-faced.

"Of course I'm happy for you," I say, and I am. My parents were rarely affectionate with each other in the best of times, and I knew that their aloofness likely carried over to the bedroom.

But now, I don't want to know, in the way that the Eight Is Enough kids didn't want to know that Dick Van Patten was fucking Betty Buckley.

Weeks later, my father takes me along to meet Maureen, an unsmiling, six-foot-tall, trench coat–wearing redhead. We go to The Sign of the Dove for lunch and stare at our pasta primavera in silence, she as uncomfortable as me, while my father makes small talk: Weather. Politics. Ed Koch. Music. Lennon and Hinckley. The three of us walk down to the MoMA, where my father buys us tickets to see Fellini's *La città della donne* (*City of Women*). The movie unfurls like a flag, stretching out endlessly in front of us: two hours of explicit sexual conquest, and Marcello Mastroianni. After the first half hour, I bolt out of the theater and sit in the lobby, and I wait for it to end. We never see Maureen again.

"Maybe he's just a serial dater," I say to Jessica, the front office manager at Sugar Maples. She's a broad, mousy blond woman who wears her hair in a dutch boy with pleated dirndl skirts and white, ruffly, puffed-sleeve blouses that button to her chin. She's whip-smart, and as warm as a bighearted German hausfrau. Thirty-one, she's recently divorced from a famous drug-addled guitarist whose band played at Woodstock.

Every Friday afternoon at three, Jessica takes a break and comes over to the snack shack for a bottle of Coke, and casually asks me the same question while I wipe down the counter.

"Is your dad bringing anyone up this weekend?"

And every Friday afternoon, I say no. Every Friday, he arrives just as dinner is being served in the main dining hall. I meet him in the lobby where he hugs me, lifting me off the ground, and then makes his way to the front desk to check in. Jessica hands him a key: the same room, every time. It takes me three weeks to notice. My father eats dinner with the owners of the hotel; as an employee, I'm relegated to the EDR, along with Steve, Emma, Jim, Jessica, and two dozen other hotel workers. We sit down together at the same time every evening, and Jim asks us to fold our hands and bow our heads: Bless this food before us set. It needs all the help that it can get.

Each night, we eat the dregs of the previous night's dining room meal: leftover pork roast reheated to the consistency of shoe leather and warmed under ladlesful of Lucky Boy canned gravy mixed with rosemary-scented melted pork fat; leftover roast beef that reappears as quasi-Salisbury steak, chopped and pounded into meaty Frisbees; leftover roast chicken ground and molded into croquettes that get deep-fried in ages-old oil that smells like trout. On every table sit two pitchers: one contains lukewarm water tasting of rusting pipes, the other, whole milk.

"Gotta go," Jessica says, as we drop our plates into the wash bin. Before everyone is done and reconvening for that night's activities— poker in someone's room; piling into someone's car to go hear Jim's band play at Channings, a nearby pub in town that ignores underage patrons—Jessica takes off for the hotel bar, where my father is reading the *New York Times* and nursing a Gibson.

THERE ARE NO RESTAURANTS IN the immediate vicinity of Sugar Maples. So when Steve decides that we all need to go out for a meal—"a formal, sit-down, grown-up dinner, with real silverware," he announces—on my last night at the hotel, our options are limited: there's Vesuvius, a small red-sauce Italian-style place in nearby Hensonville that my father has taken me to a few times over the summer.

"Forget it," Steve says, shaking his head. "They know my parents."

We're sitting in the empty snack shack on a rainy late August Friday afternoon; Emma mops the linoleum back-room floor while Steve and I sit at one of the front tables with two massive stacks of cold cuts, a thick sheaf of white deli paper cut into six-inch squares, and a scale. I separate the meat and cheese into three-ounce packages for sandwiches with coy names like Ham and Cheese Wouldya Please, which is ham and cheese on rye, and Little Orphan Hammy, which is ham on white, no cheese, no mayo, no mustard. When a guest wants more meat or cheese on his sandwich, I have to charge him more, per slice. The ham—it is not technically Black Forest or honey-roasted but rather just plain ham—comes mechanically formed and shrink-wrapped into the shape of a shoe box. I spend hours running it through the whirring metal slicing machine and stacking it; the two-foot-high tower of boiled, pressed meat reminds me of the Danish stuff Inga used to serve to my mother in Forest Hills, back before she and Eddie, Tor, and George moved. While I'm weighing the ham, I think of Gaga at home in her apartment, watching the Yankees, and Grandma Bertha in Brooklyn, cleaning the kitchen and getting ready to light her Shabbos candles, and a wave of guilt knocks the wind out of me.

"Hey," Steve says, kicking my chair. "Did you hear me? Where else? Emma—" he yells, turning around, "where else?"

"You're the local, dumbass," she yells back, ringing out her mop in a galvanized steel bucket.

We pile into two cars and end up at The Stewart House, a bed-and-breakfast three towns away. Steve, wearing khakis, a button-down oxford cloth shirt, and a clip-on tie that barely reaches his navel, sits at the head of the table, and Emma plants herself directly opposite him in the one flowered silk hippy dress she rolled up into a ball and stuffed into her bag when she packed to come to the hotel for the summer. Eric sits next to me and his girlfriend, Sally, next to him. Jim the Yardbird joins us, along with Jack Doherty's little sister, Carla; and Barbara, who works in the office with Jessica, comes along, too. We're seated in the inn's private dining room, which is illuminated by a fake gas-powered chandelier dripping with cut crystals. Our server, a gum-cracking, acne-scarred woman wearing a name tag that says Call Me Colleen, refuses Steve's request for the wine list; the only one at the table technically old enough to drink is Jim, who orders a Coke. Platters begin to arrive—spaghetti and meatballs, Caesar salad, garlic bread, chicken Kiev, peas and carrots, fried zucchini—and the din in the room begins to rise; the server closes the french doors that separate us from the rest of the inn.

"To you," Steve play-acts, dramatically thrusting his goblet of Sprite in my direction and kicking me hard under the table. He is the make-believe man of our house; it's as if he's playing dress-up in his father's clothes. He is carefree; I know nothing about his past or his home life. Perhaps he is beaten every night at seven by an alcoholic father who he's desperate to escape until one night, the man, with visions of a 1968 attack near Quang Tri Province, lunges at his thin, sleeping boy with a knife, and the boy, now tall as a man, overtakes his father and throws him out into the Catskills mountain snow, to sleep it off. Perhaps not. Perhaps Emma had gotten pregnant at Exeter, and abandoned by her parents, left school and looked for work. Perhaps not. Whoever we are, we came to the table at The Stewart

House with no past; we didn't ask, and we didn't want to know. We were fresh, newly minted near-adults, psychic virgins with no prejudices or rages, who could only look forward to the future with hope.

"To us," I answer quietly—this is what they say in movies, I think—looking around the table at this motley crew of strangers who have, in the midst of my chaotic life, become my family.

When the check arrives, we all pull wads of singles out of our pockets, except for Emma, who puts her father's Diner's Club card on the table; Steve leaves his share of the tip in pennies he carried to the restaurant in a zip-lock sandwich bag.

WE SKULKED BACK TO OUR rooms not through the lobby, but up the fire escape that ran along the outside of the building; as I climbed it, I see my father and Jessica sitting at a small table in the corner of the bar. He smokes; she rests her hand on top of his.

Steve stayed in my room that night; when we got in, he yanked off his tie and unbuttoned his shirt, and we spent hours sitting on the floor of my room and talking about high school and college and the primal need to escape Maplecrest and Forest Hills, and hours rolling around on the floor, a groaning pile of disembodied arms and legs. At two in the morning, exhausted and sweaty, I threw on Steve's shirt and got up to use the bathroom at the other end of the hallway. The floors creaked under my bare feet; I could hear voices coming from a room near the bathroom, and when my eyes adjusted to the darkness, I had to squint to make out the vague outline of a familiar figure. My father crept out of Jessica's room and quietly pulled her door closed.

"Dad," I whispered.

"Shit—" he said, giggling like a drunk teenager. "Caught me." "Jessica?" I looked over his shoulder towards her room.

He sheepishly shook his head yes; he gazed past me and down the hall towards my room, and smiled.

We drove home to Forest Hills the next day in silence. "Anything you want to tell me?" he said, staring straight ahead as we weaved and snaked south along the tree-lined Taconic State Parkway. I gazed out the window.

"Steve?"

A cloud of green blurred along outside; I didn't answer. "Or Emma?"

PART III

How shall we sing the Lord's song in a strange land?

—Psalms 137:4

The transformation of the heart is a wondrous thing,
no matter how you land there.

—Patti Smith, *M Train*

19

602

FAMILY LORE:

My father was nine when a neighbor living across the street on the south side of Ocean Parkway offered Grandpa Henry first crack at the redbrick 1920s Spanish-style house he was putting up for sale because he was moving to California. Clay mission-roofed and pristinely landscaped with abundant white climbing roses scaling a thick cedar trellis covering the carport and mature rhododendrons with deep fuchsia blossoms flanking the transom, the house took up nearly a quarter of the square city block. The el train rumbled by only a few streets away, but the house was lush and alive and throbbing with the promise of suburbia, and it stood out among the parkway's squat, eraser-pink apartment buildings as though it had fallen abruptly from the sky like a satellite traveling west on its way to Pasadena.

My grandfather, the story went, yearned for that house and all that it meant: he envisioned his children and grandchildren running safely around the fenced-in yard, shielded from the grime and din of

Brooklyn. He imagined Talmud study sessions with the local rabbis over his wife's gorgeous kosher dinners prepared in a modern kitchen big enough for two stoves and two sinks and two iceboxes. But it was 1934, the effects of the Depression lingered on like a vague hallway odor, and the $25,000 price that Jay Silverheels asked was simply too steep. So my grandfather chose to stay in the two-bedroom apartment with the rippling, faux stucco walls that he shared with Grandma Bertha, my father, and Aunt Sylvia; the house across the street became a tantalizing dream and a symbol of what could have been, like the model homes my father would take my mother and me to visit every weekend when I was a child. In what was my grandparents' first brush with Hollywood royalty—but not their last: they ran into Jayne Mansfield during the Rose Parade when my father drove them cross-country in 1948; when he saw her, my grandfather shouted, Hey, Janie baby, and my father said she turned around and blew him a kiss—they turned down the man who played Tonto and remained at 602 Avenue T for the rest of their lives.

Besides walk-to-worship, the apartment's allure was dubious; it wasn't the view, although the east-facing bedrooms where my grandfather prayed morning and night were cooled by soft eastern breezes blowing in off Coney Island, and on a clear day you could see the Parachute Drop and the merchant tankers floating along on the glimmering bay in the distance. My grandmother's prized Knabe baby grand piano stood in the dark living room adjacent to the south window and flush against a steam radiator that howled and clanged in the winter and stayed hot and damp regardless of the season; eventually, the piano's mahogany veneer finish peeled and fissured and its ivory keys crazed like fine porcelain. By the time I moved to 602 Avenue T in 1991, the posterboard rendering of Bruegel's *The Harvesters* that hung above the sofa bulged out of its frame, making the field hands look like ghosts on a Mathew Brady battlefield.

My family called the apartment 602—just 602—like a three-digit secret code for our past. After my grandmother died in her sleep there at ninety-three, my father and Aunt Sylvia left everything in place—except for the good silver and the crystal and a few pieces of jewelry—where it had stood for almost sixty years; the apartment became a shrine. When I got there, it was like cracking open a time capsule: assorted bric-a-brac and small china statues from Aunt Sylvia's frequent trips to Europe and South America remained where I remembered them standing nearly three decades earlier, on the end tables flanking the couch. My grandfather's vast, dust-caked, leather-bound Yiddish library sat untouched in the mahogany living room breakfront, bookended by two mother-of-pearl, life-size magpies in flight. Photos of my father and Uncle Lee in their World War II uniforms were displayed on the piano, alongside a high school graduation picture of a stunning, teenage Aunt Sylvia shot in the late 1930s, and two eight-by-tens of my older cousins, taken when they were in college in the 1960s. As a child, I had never noticed it; as an adult, it made me wince: at 602, there was no discernible sign of my presence in my grandparents' lives.

Nothing about the apartment had changed: not the original nameplate from 1933—H. Altman, it said, in a swirling art deco font of the time—slipped into the little slot under the front door peep hole. The phone was still connected with the apartment's original number—ESsex 5-1177—in the assumption, or maybe just the hope, that someone might still try to call. On the bitterly cold January day when the apartment became mine, I tried to unpack my suitcases, but couldn't: my grandparents' clothes—paisley Qiana dresses; a gold polyester bed jacket from a 1970ish hospital visit to remove an angry appendix; a white stole of unidentifiable fur; six fine wool suits in various shades of steel gray, size 42 regular; neatly pressed button-down dress shirts and striped rep ties and leather belts—hung in the closets as though my grandparents still lived there. Both beds were tidily made: my grandfather's massive horsehair mattress in the big, east-facing bedroom, and my grandmother's narrow single bed, in what had been my father and Aunt Sylvia's childhood bedroom. In the bathroom, a matted thicket of frosted hair cocooned my grandmother's favorite Mason Pearson brush, which sat in the medicine cabinet above the flesh-toned sink, next to a rusting container of Colgate tooth powder. Her flowered makeup bag gaped open on a small putty-colored stool near the tub, holding the things that made her beautiful: Coty blush in frosted peach, a crumbling cake of dusty brown mascara like a square of old chocolate, a pot of Revlon powder blue eye shadow. I touched my finger to the lipstick—Max Factor Misty Coral—and then to my mouth; it tasted stale, like last Halloween's wax lips.

In the kitchen, where nearly two decades earlier, I had been fed a cold boiled brain, the glossy white ceiling-high cabinets, painted and painted and repainted again until they refused to close, were filled with my grandmother's coffee cups and saucers, juice glasses, and the repurposed 1940s yahrzeit memorial candle glasses that she saved over the years and used as perfect ten-ounce measuring cups. In a drawer, I found a three-pound Koch Messer—a giant meat cleaver, its blade dull as butter, carried over on the boat from Romania by my great-grandmother—buried under a pile of Maxwell House Passover Haggadahs. The 1950s refrigerator—a squat, bulbous Frigidaire with a massive metal handle that hugged its wide midsection like a girdle—still plugged in, hummed, and belched near the kitchen table. I pulled the door open carefully, expecting to be overcome by a wave of rotted food; instead, a moist, dank cloud of mildew wafted out and into the kitchen, dissipating as it made its way to the open window. Inside the fridge stood a half-empty container of two-year-old Mother's gefilte fish next to an old mayonnaise bottle covered with disintegrating wax paper secured with a wide red rubber band; although the contents was now a rancid gray swamp, I recognized it as my grandmother's favorite griebenes jar. An open box of her favorite Coffee Nips stood on the foyer telephone table next to the brown paisley upholstered French provincial chair from which she liked to watch *The Muppet Show* in the 1980s.

When my grandmother died, fifteen years after her husband, life at 602 had been simply placed on hold, like a staticky phone call; the fact that she wasn't coming home seemed impossible to her children.

• • •

EACH OF US HAS AN immediate, olfactory connection to our grandparents, who emit the musty clouds of age; hallways and bedrooms smell like dust, or mothballs, or liniment. In my case, they smelled like food, and my connection to them grew during the weekend mornings of my childhood, when my parents and I walked into the lobby at 602, which reeked, perpetually, of chicken fat.

For years, the building's resident super was a Hasidic rabbi named Lipshitz who regularly took long, ambling afternoon walks down Ocean Parkway with his young wife and their eight daughters in tow. Lipshitz, who my grandfather detested—Lipshitz the Goniff, he called him—was still there when I, the building's last tenant whose legal right to rent the apartment fell under the archaic rules of New York City real estate law, moved in. When we passed each other in the lobby, Lipshitz glared at me from head to toe like treyf—unkosher, unacceptable, unclean—since I didn't have to gain his approval before taking up residence. Everyone else in the building was ultra-Orthodox and had been since the building was built; that many people cooking that much griebenes under one roof for more than sixty years had taken its toll. Although Lipshitz took pride in the sparkling cleanliness of the hallways and the lobby, over time, the essence of schmaltz had been sucked into the pores of the place. When I moved in, the building still reeked; I feared for my clothes. I was certain that my two cats would stink like a pair of fat Shabbos pullets.

"Can't anything be done about the smell?" I asked Lipshitz when I handed over my first check for the $142 a month rent. He took it from me gingerly, like I was a leper.

"Maybe you could get out," he said, shrugging. "Nobody wants you here anyway."

I looked at him in silent rage; this man from the old country, this specter from the past, wanted me gone, banished from his building like it was his own personal shtetl.

But I didn't want me there either; it had been a last resort. Cheap rent, a few blocks from the subway, a place for me to get my bearings after a bad breakup.

"We own it in perpetuity," my father promised me when I began to receive regular notices of eviction from the building owner, who wanted to turn it into a co-op like the rest of the apartments in 602; 5H was the last rental holdout.

"We don't own it, Dad—I'm paying monthly rent."

"You'll stay and bring your husband and raise your children there," my father explained matter-of-factly while we were in the car, driving to housing court in downtown Brooklyn; he was counting on it, although Lipshitz was evicting me, to free up the apartment for sale.

"Are you delusional?" I gasped, looking over at him. "I have to return to my life in the city. I'm never going to live here permanently."

He pulled over into a bus stop and glared at me.

"There has been an Altman here since 1933," he said, his face beginning to flush a deep red. "You are the last one. This is our family home, our connection to the past, to who we once were. It is your responsibility to maintain that connection."

I opened up the passenger door, unbuckled my seat belt, and vomited into the street.

Like my father, who had returned to his childhood apartment after he divorced my mother, I went to 602 to heal my wounds; like him, I had nowhere else to go.

THERE HAD BEEN A BEAUTIFUL, petite medical resident from Minnesota, who I will call Julie. When we met, I was dating men, and sleeping with a tall, long-haired advertising creative director named James; he wore tiny round wire-rimmed glasses that seemed to always slide down his aquiline nose; wide, colorful ties from the early 1950s; and, on the weekends, a collection of moth-eaten Shetland sweaters from Goodwill. The food we ate in the late 1980s was tall and fancy and soulless, and sex was perfunctory and mechanical. Still, I loved the neutralizing idea of him if not exactly him; when he left me alone in his Greenwich Village bedroom every Sunday morning to play soccer in Central Park with a bunch of Guatemalan boys ten years his junior, I relished my quiet time alone to read the paper and drink endless cups of dark English tea before going back to the Upper West Side apartment I shared with my mother and Ben, who she married in 1981, and where I slept in the den every night on their beige pullout sofa that possessed all the comfort of a torture device invented by Torquemada.

Julie was taking a summer break from her orthopedic residency to work for my Greenwich Village physician. She shared her squalid, mouse-laden walkup tenement apartment near the hospital with a colonic-addicted anorexic vegan nutritionist who wore her black hair in the style of Medusa; Julie wanted out of her situation. So did I. We became roommates, decorating the tiny, white-bricked Chelsea flat we illegally subletted from the X-ray technician in her office with Native American dream catchers and crystals of every shape and variety: Julie promised me that if I closed my eyes and quieted my brain, I could feel the heat coming off a rose quartz orb that we'd spent a week's salary on, and that it would ease the broken heart she was sure I had been carrying if not in this life, then certainly in past ones. A smoky quartz pyramid was going to guarantee our success at our life-work—hers as a physician, mine, I hoped, as a novelist. A hunk of watermelon tourmaline, dug, we were told, from a watermelon tourmaline mine in Pakistan, would transmute our negative energies and attract love, which it did: after three months of sleeping in separate rooms, we were gifted the keys to a friend's New Hampshire cottage, where we spent her Christmas break. As Interstate 91 snaked through Hartford and Springfield and into Vermont, it began to flurry; when we crossed the White River into Hanover, it started to snow. By the time we reached the cottage, flakes like half dollars blanketed and then shut down the state; for ten days, we stayed under the covers, wrapped around each other. Sex was tender and delicious and we fell asleep in each other's arms. We lost track of time and day and morning and night, exhausted and weeping with explosive relief and the slow burn of terror that comes from the fulfillment of the illicit.

When we returned to New York, I moved in to her bedroom. We told no one. At Christmas, we decorated the tiny tree I had always secretly lusted for like many Jewish children—I told my father it was Julie's when he came over for dinner and glared at it—with cheap, folk art ornaments we bought by the handful at the Pearl River Market in SoHo: there were Santas made from wooden blocks, angels fashioned from cornstalks, snowflakes macraméed in glittery silver polyester.

We played house; I craved the peace and happiness I found in Gaga's kitchen, and I was certain that if I cooked, I would find it—I would find her—again. During Thanksgiving, we stuffed pumpkins with vegetables procured from the Union Square farmers' market and roasted them for our friends in New Hampshire; they exploded in the oven and dripped their innards all over our friends' newly stripped heart pine floor. We threw dinner parties and brunches and one Saturday night became chanting Buddhists at a crowded apartment gathering on Avenue C, where we were separated from each other the minute we arrived; a rail-thin man whose exuberance could only be attributed to huge amounts of cocaine, thrust into my hand a sheet of paper containing the primary chant that, if I did it correctly, would give me anything I wanted.

"Really," he said, emphatically. "Anything. You just have to do it loud. You could get anything. Even a new car."

Four years later, it was over: anguished with Lutheran guilt that no amount of positive energy from her glimmering forest of crystals that covered our living room could stifle, Julie began to bring men home. I moved out to the couch, which backed up to her bedroom wall; for six months, I slept curled up in a fetal position between our two blond wood Conran end tables crowded as a subway car with massive geodic chunks of purple amethyst and citrine quartz and a wooden bowl filled with the Herkimer diamonds that were guaranteed to clear the electromagnetic pollution in our living room; I meditated to Shakti Gawain's Creative Visualization tapes on my Walkman while Julie fucked her way through Manhattan on the other side of the wall. I closed my eyes and visualized what I wanted: I wanted us to be a happy family. I imagined having dinner around a long pine rectory table with our perfect little towheaded children, celebrating birthdays and holidays with massive standing ribs of beefs and special, peanut-fed Virginia hams; I visualized vacations on Martha's Vineyard and lobster boils around burning campfires on the beach near Menemsha. I could taste the promise of sustenance and peace and happiness away from my history, away from my past, the way a junkie tastes smack, as if our life together was clipped from the Martha Stewart magazines that piled up in every corner of our apartment. Ours would be spent together in celebration, at the table, like the family I was certain we would be. And no matter what I saw on the great slide show of my brain, when I opened my eyes and took off my headphones, Julie was still on the other side of the wall, fucking every man who walked into her life.

BOXES WERE CRAMMED INTO MY grandparents' living room from end to end.

A mountain of cookbooks in moving company cartons sat piled in front of the windows, where my grandmother's piano had stood until right before I arrived, when it had been refurbished and shipped off to a cousin whose daughter was just starting to take lessons. Edna Lewis, Julia Child, Paula Wolfert, Deborah Madison, Richard Olney, Jane Grigson, Marcella Hazan, Madeleine Kamman, Alice Waters, Felipe Rojas-Lombardi, Christopher Idone, Mollie Katzen, and the splattered pages of Laurel's Kitchen were jammed together like sardines, the result of my two years as a book department manager at Dean & DeLuca, where I spent twelve hours a day trying to help customers inevitably replicate some version of their past at the table.

"I want it to be just like it was when I was a kid," they'd say, and I knew what that meant: I searched for Gaga in the kitchen. So together, we'd search the shelves to help them find just the thing that might enable them to re-create their favorite childhood Christmas dinner, had Daddy not gotten drunk and passed out face-first into the wassail before the roast was carved. Or the Passover seder where Grandma dumped a Waterford goblet of Manischewitz on the section of the Haggadah about the matriarchs and the patriarchs. One famous SoHo art dealer, who wore heavy black Wayfarers on top of her shoulder-length ginger perm, wanted to re-create her beatnik mother's lentil nut loaf, which she remembered eating while wearing Dr. Denton's and watching *The Donna Reed Show*.

"It was the only time," she blithely whispered to me like I was her new best friend, "that Papi wasn't beating on me." She pulled a copy of *The Vegetarian Epicure* off the shelf, tucked it into her shopping basket along with a twelve-dollar bag of ebony beluga lentils, said, "Ta-ta," and was on her way.

The world careened around us; it imploded, fell apart, turned angry and uncontrollable, and at the table, everything could be fixed and made whole the way it had been for me ten years earlier at a lackluster hotel in the middle of upstate New York, surrounded by people I barely knew; it was there that I discovered the inviolability of sharing food together—"the modern tribal fire," Marion Cunningham once called it—even if there was no DNA involved.

The table could sometimes breed violence and it could be the backdrop to the proscribed and the forbidden and the perverse, the way it had been the night my mother blacked out her tooth at the Tung Shing House. But feeding people made them happy; it made me happy, and grounded me. I had not been able to get home to say goodbye to Gaga, but doing for others what she had done for me—providing me with sustenance and love—kept her alive. Food filled our hearts as well as our bellies, and it pacified our soul. There was Edna Lewis's boiled pork shoulder, which I made one Easter when Julie's family came east from Edina; Richard Olney's chicken gratin, which I packed up and carried to my boss's apartment, clear across the city, when his mother died suddenly and he was too bereft to think about cooking; Deborah Madison's baked polenta with fontina, which I made when Julie became a vegetarian and I, desperately in love with her, became one, too. There was Anna Thomas's thick, earthy chestnut soup, which I fed to twenty friends at a vegan Thanksgiving dinner in Woodstock around a farmhouse table long enough to serve the Osmond family. And there was Alice Waters' lobster mousse vinaigrette, which I presented to my mother and Ben at their apartment in matte black champagne flutes, each one accompanied by a massive boiled prawn hooked over the side of the glass like an umbrella handle, while they just stared at me.

Cooking became my religion, the key to my sacred, the path to sanctity and peace.

In front of the boxes of books sat cartons of cookware: a set of heavy, tin-lined, cast-iron-handled copper that I'd collected in individual pieces and hung off a pot rack from the white brick kitchen wall of my Chelsea apartment; an aluminum fish poacher I used on the infrequent catering jobs I took to offset my pathetic retail salary; muffin tins and black iron half-sheet pans and egg poachers and a vinyl roll holding fifteen knives I'd amassed over the years of cooking for myself and for anyone who I could get to sit still long enough. Food became the air that I breathed, my right foot in front of my left, the wall around the side of the pool that I clung to to keep from getting sucked down and under. It took the place of Gaga herself.

But at 602, my knives, my cookware, my cookbooks—my tools of sustenance and safety and peace—would remain packed for the eighteen months I lived in my grandmother's apartment.

THE FIRST NIGHT I STAYED alone at the apartment, my father's phone call set off the ringer amplifiers that he'd left attached to the ceiling in every room—my grandmother had gone stone deaf in her later years—and when he checked in on me, the walls and windows shook and my cats shrieked and hid in the bowels of the coat closet. He was calling, he said, to give me some advice.

"Whatever you do," he said, "don't turn on the stove."

"What if I want to cook?" I said.

I stood in the foyer, in front of my grandmother's Sony Trinitron, sucking down a glass of the Bombay Sapphire gin that my father had deposited on the kitchen shelf next to a rusting 1947 Tzedakah box raising money for the new State of Israel, after dropping me off.

"Use the top burners, but never more than two at a time. And don't light the oven. I'll take you to Macy's tomorrow to buy a microwave."

I was suddenly single, alone after a bad breakup, living in my long-dead grandparents' apartment with all of their things—their clothes, their pictures, their hairbrushes, their lipstick—and I couldn't even roast myself a chicken without blowing the place up. I couldn't bake a pie or a loaf of bread. I couldn't broil a piece of salmon or make a lasagna or a brisket or oven-braise root vegetables or a leg of lamb. I couldn't make a frittata or a pizza or brownies or a pork roast.

I couldn't even bake a potato.

We went to Macy's the next night, and my father bought me a microwave big enough to be an end table.

"There's a roast chicken setting," he said, pointing to its front panel. We took it back to 602, plugged it in, heated up a mug of water, and instantly blew one of the two fuses that powered the entire apartment. Lights flickered. A popping sound and a faint whiff of electrical smoke filled the air and we stood in the kitchen in our winter coats and stared at each other in silence, not knowing what to do, like two children.

"We should go out," he said.

We went to a nearby Chinese restaurant called Karr's; we ate at a small table near the bar and got drunk on gin Gibsons.

"So where do I buy food?" I asked him over a platter of pork-fried rice.

Julie had been a selective vegetarian; I once found a mustard-stained Gray's Papaya hot dog napkin in her jeans pocket while I was doing the laundry. When I brought home a porterhouse, she said that I was judging her, and that was the beginning of the end. I couldn't be any more a vegetarian than a hyena on a kill, and from the point where our relationship ended, I gorged myself, happily and willingly, on enough meat to feed an army. I filled our freezer with Manhattan strips and lamb chops, petite fillets and veal breasts and skirt steaks. And pork: enormous quantities of pork. Every time I cooked one, Julie lit a sage smudge stick, waved it around my head, and prayed for the soul of the animal I just ate.

Sitting at Karr's with my father, I plucked the dark red cubes of hong shao rou, familiar to me from our Sunday night dinners at the Tung Shing House, from between a tangle of sprouts and slivered carrots and celery and I ate them one by one.

"There's King's Highway," he said, shoveling shrimp and lobster sauce onto his plate.

"Is there anything closer?"

"Avenue U. Near the F train. Your grandmother never went there."

"Why not?" "Italian."

Grandma Bertha once stole a piece of bacon from my breakfast plate when my father brought her up to Boston to visit me at college. She ate steamed lobster at The Jolly Fisherman on Long Island, during Aunt Sylvia and Uncle Lee's family gatherings. She ate prawn cocktails and ham and Swiss sandwiches and cheeseburgers. But 602—where my grandfather had raged and my father had longed for love and Aunt Sylvia silently planned to live a different kind of ordered, beautiful life—was off-limits to anything that hadn't been prayed over, sanctified, and koshered, as if the very roof over their heads was tenuous, and hanging by a slender, fraying thread directly connected to God.

Avenue U was a four-block walk from 602; there were no taxis or buses involved in getting there. But during my first week in the apartment, it didn't matter, because I didn't cook. After work on a Friday night, I came back to the apartment starving for pizza, and ordered a pie from a nearby pizzeria; Lipshitz gasped when the delivery guy passed him in the hallway carrying the grease-stained, white cardboard box with the word "SAUSAGE" stamped on its side. I ordered cartons of Szechuan pork from a local Chinese takeout place and ate them at my grandparents' flowered oilcloth-covered kitchen table with the Parachute Drop hovering behind me out the window; I dumped the clumps of cheap, double-fried meat onto a mountain of steamed white rice I'd spooned onto my grandmother's magenta-flowered brain plate, and shared the dinner table with the smudged, black-and-white pictures of the marching Israeli children that wrapped around her Tzedakah box and stood dusty and forgotten on a corner cupboard shelf since she began stuffing them with folded-up dollar bills after the war was over. I put my fork down and shook the box; it rattled like a maraca, noisy with hope.

A WEEK AFTER MOVING IN, I got sick with the kind of flu that makes you want to die: the kind where every joint aches and your fever spikes and every orifice is clogged and stuffed like a drain, and any sense of smell or taste is flattened and it no longer matters what you eat because it might as well be a couch cushion. When the moving van left, I had dragged my suitcase into my grandfather's bedroom for the east-facing windows and the breezes that I would get in the spring and summer; I slept on the crinkling, horsehair mattress where I had hallucinated years earlier, when the painting of my long-dead cousin had come alive and stepped out of her frame and swirled around me in voluminous ballet skirts before climbing back into the past. When the flu hit, I retreated to the massive bed and stayed there for days, until a dull ache in my stomach reminded me I had to eat. Feverish and achy, I pulled on a sweatshirt and jeans and stumbled across Ocean Parkway towards Avenue U. I found myself navigating a wall of marching, tight-lipped, unsmiling older women pulling empty grocery carts behind them. I followed them south, under the elevated F train, to the Italian neighborhood where my grandmother never went.

There was a cheese shop and a tiny greengrocer selling baskets of fresh fava beans and bunches of spicy, bitter puntarelle. There was a pork and sausage store that also sold fresh and dried pasta, and massive, round cans of salted Sicilian anchovies; a bakery selling fresh semolina bread dotted with sesame seeds; a fishmonger; a butcher whose window display included ducks with their heads on, chickens with their feet attached, and rabbits that had been skinned down to the circles of fur around their feet, like the booties on Phyllis Diller. The women with the pushcarts methodically popped in and out of the stores; they ordered loudly, paid for their groceries, and moved on.

Hoarse, I asked the cheese man for taleggio, my favorite soft creamy northern Italian washed-rind cheese that emits such a stink that it could peel wallpaper; he shook his head no. An older, gray-haired lady wearing a jet-black cardigan, jet-black wool skirt, and suntan panty hose eyed me up and down with a grimace, like I'd just flown in from Mars.

"Don't go anywhere," the cheese man ordered. "Just wait a minute."

He disappeared into the back of the store and a few minutes later returned with a demitasse cup, which he passed to me over a massive wheel of provolone sitting on the counter.

"Drink it all at once—you'll feel better. Come back tomorrow. I close at six."

A scrim had been lifted, and the sepia world I was living in was suddenly brilliant with color. Every day, I did my shopping on Avenue U, and every day, the little old Italian ladies in black grilled me about what I was making and how I was making it. Sometimes they nodded in approval and asked me where I lived, and whether I was single, because they had a nice grandson. Often, they corrected me. When I said I couldn't bake anything because the oven might explode, they shook fingers in my face and said, "You don't need an oven." I imagined Gaga, her mouth pulled into a thin line of anger and practicality.

At the pork store and the greengrocer, I bought anything I could cook on top of the stove: there were thick coils of fennel and garlic sausage that I simmered with red wine, grapes, and thyme, and then seared in a hot skillet; fava beans that I boiled and shelled and mashed into a topping for the semolina bread that I toasted in my grandmother's oil-slicked cast-iron frying pan, and then rubbed with garlic; I wilted the bitter puntarelle in a pot of salted, boiling water, and tossed it with orecchiette cooked in the vegetable water, and folded giant spoonfuls of thick, fatty sheep's milk ricotta into the warm pasta. In the coming eighteen months, I left my cookware packed in boxes in the living room and raided my grandmother's dusty cupboards: her ancient aluminum pots clattered on the stovetop, their bottoms rounded and dimpled with age. I crushed garlic with my great-grandmother's Koch Messer, which I could barely lift; I steamed what needed steaming in a white enameled colander set over a small pot of boiling water; I wine-braised butterflied pigeon in my grandmother's old Teflon matzo brei fry pan covered with a warped cookie sheet; I dredged branzino in seasoned egg and flour and slid it into a hot, buttercoated oval metal casserole from the 1930s that had baked decades of kugels; I drank cheap red wine out of the tiny four-ounce milk glasses of my childhood Sunday lunches; I drizzled warm, quartered figs with the dregs of my grandfather's Slivovitz that I found sitting in the depths of the hall closet, buried behind torn Klein's of Fourteenth Street shopping bags bursting with the fading letters that my father had written to his parents from the Pacific during World War II when he was nineteen.

I cooked for myself every night and had my dinners alone at the kitchen table, surrounded by the ghosts of the people who had fed me brains and borscht, and who said, You'll eat it, even as my young throat tightened and the food of the past made me ill. Every night for eighteen months, I ate my dinner while sifting through piles of dog-eared photographs of long-forgotten cousins in Europe, of my acne-pocked teenage father who longed for his own father's affection, of my grandparents on the beach in Coney Island in 1917 right after they were married, of my great-grandmother in Novyy Yarchev right before the Nazis came.

602 was where I went to steady myself, to relearn who I was and exactly what I had become: When I moved out—when it was time to get back to my life—I took nothing with me: not the Koch Messer or the Slivovitz, the time-warped Bruegel or the juice glasses. I left with my cats and my clothes and my cookbooks—still sealed in their moving boxes from the day I arrived—and tucked the stash of my father's wartime letters into my knapsack. On my way out, I stopped into the kitchen and picked up my grandmother's old Tzedakah box, which I had been using as a paperweight against the breezes coming in off Coney Island; beneath it was the sheaf of wrinkled, handwritten kitchen notes that I'd scrawled, some on the backs of envelopes, while standing in the stores on Avenue U with the stern-faced Italian

ladies. I stuffed the notes into my bag and left the Tzedakah box where I'd found it when I moved in, like a sentinel.

The old refrigerator heaved a death rattle when I reached behind the damp, cool coils and pulled the plug out of the wall. I turned the lights off, stepped out into the hallway, and closed the door behind me; I reached up and touched the mezuzah, attached by my grandfather sixty years earlier, and said goodbye.

20

The Dead File

UNTIL HE MOVED OUT, and for all the years of my childhood, my father kept his copy of *The Rise and Fall of the Third Reich* on the top shelf of the Danish modern étagère in our living room in The Marseilles, sandwiched between *Portnoy's Complaint* and an ebony bust of the Buddha. They sat there until I was fifteen, gathering dust, when my father left and took his books with him. For years, my father would point up at them and I'd stare at the shelf with benign curiosity, and all he would say was "They're not for you." It was a game we played, like cat and mouse; we both knew the rules, which we never spoke.

"What's in them?" I would answer, poking at him like a bear. All of his other stuff was within my reach: the Cheever, the Updike, the Vidal, the Mailer, the *Playboys*, the *Reader's Digest* abridged editions.

"Never mind," he'd say.

"But why can't I see them?" I'd ask. "Forbidden," he'd say.

"But why?" I'd whine.

"If I wanted you to reach them, they wouldn't be up there, would they?" he'd say.

I'd stand in the living room, my head tilted back far as though I was having a tooth drilled, and wonder why, exactly, they were off-limits.

When I was very young, the fact of the books didn't matter—I couldn't have read them anyway, so their being dangled in front of me like Tantalus's grapes was gratuitous and maybe a tiny bit cruel: tell a child that they can't have something—a snack, a toy, a book—and they are instantly drawn to it. By the time I was in grade school, I had heard enough dinner party stories about the Nazis and whole families hidden in attics being taken out and shot in the streets to believe that, as a Jewish girl, I could likely expect the same fate; I assumed that violence would be a part of my life simply because of who I was. I wouldn't have read the Third Reich book even if I had been able to reach it. I wouldn't have needed to; I knew the story by heart.

By the time I got to middle school—fending off Tor Hoffmann's humping and Buck's pawing at me in the front seat of his '62 Falcon and Lisa Epstein passing around her diaphragm on the school bus—I would have been repulsed by Portnoy, who fucked the family dinner two hours before everyone sat down to the table to eat it, but I wouldn't have been shocked.

I never got near my father's illicit reading material; he kept it away from me because of its atrocity on the one hand and its mastur-batory gravitas on the other. But he also wanted me to know it was there, and a part of life. But I didn't need to read them: I knew about Nazis from the stories he told me, and from Judith Garbfeld, who had killed her first soldier when she was seven. And I knew about the underside of sex—its shame, its perversion, its power to manipulate and control and terrify—because Buck, on our quiet Friday after-noon hikes while Gaga was home slicing the potatoes for our Shab-bos supper—had shown it to me.

Still, I wanted to know what was in the books I couldn't reach not because I was interested in their contents. I wanted to know about them because I wanted to hear the words directly from my father, without suggestion or innuendo; I wanted to hear him tell me exactly what gives birth to brutality, and exactly where shame comes from. And I wanted to understand how perpetrators of cruelty live with themselves as the world spins around them. I wanted to know what he believed stopped them, who we had to talk to or pray to.

MY FATHER FOISTED HIS OTHER favorite books on me when I was a child; there was Carl Sandburg's three-volume Abraham Lincoln when I was eight, John Updike's *Rabbit, Run* when I was ten, and his beloved Lion Feuchtwanger's Weimar-era novel, *Jew Süss,* when I was eleven. He marched into my bedroom carrying whatever it was that he wanted to share with me that week, and he'd leave it on my dresser or my bed, sometimes with a note written in the same tiny, tense script that had appeared in his letters home from the Navy. It said:

Read it and then we'll talk about it. Dad

"So what did you think?" he asked me one night after dinner, pointing to the Feuchtwanger sitting on my little white, pinkflowered children's desk. I'd mindlessly buried the book underneath a pile of David Cassidy fan magazines, hoping my father would somehow forget that he'd given it to me, which he did not.

"I mean, you read it, didn't you?"

"I'm not done with it yet," I lied, my hands stuffed deep into the pockets of my Wranglers.

"So what part are you up to, exactly?" he asked, folding his arms across his chest. He bent his head down and glared at me over the top of his aviators, which was what he did when he wanted to extract an admission of guilt.

"I don't know," I muttered.

Ssssss, he breathed through his teeth like a steam engine. He shook his head in disappointment, pulled the book out from underneath the magazines, and walked out of my room carrying it tucked underneath his arm.

He didn't speak to me for a week. At first I thought it was my imagination, and when he passed me in the hallway and I said, Good morning, Dad, and he turned his head away from me and kept going, I realized it wasn't.

"Why aren't you talking to me?" I asked him over dinner that night. There was plain broiled salmon steak, flaccid canned asparagus; no rice, no potatoes, no bread. My father drank his Dewar's, my mother her Soave, and I, Hawaiian Punch out of a tiki mug that Gaga sent away for by mailing in ten Hawaiian Punch can labels.

No response; I asked again.

Our little black-and-white television blared *The Price Is Right* from where it sat at the end of the table next to my mother, who was picking at her food.

"You know why," he answered, staring at the set. He sighed heavily, breathing hard with exasperation.

"I don't know why," I said.

"I'm sure you'll figure it out," he said, standing up and dumping his plate and glass in the sink. He slipped the leather collar onto our dog and walked out of the apartment, letting the door slam behind him.

"He's not talking to me?" I asked my mother. She looked up from her plate.

"He'll get over it," she said, turning back to the television. Over dinner, the situation had become clear: his disappointment became my abandonment, ignited by a minor transgression. It felt rational in my house, and a normal response to benign disobedience: the hoary threat of desertion for reasons that no one could identify was wielded like a scimitar.

Decades later, after he died, I found a long-overdue library book among my father's things, checked out years earlier with the obvious intention of never returning it. *Jew Süss* by Lion Feuchtwanger, the book that he so desperately wanted me to read when I was a child, was sitting in his office closet in the Long Island condo he shared with his longtime girlfriend, hidden on a shelf beneath his royal blue velvet tallis bag. The story of an eighteenth-century wealthy Jewish businessman-turned-political advisor to the Duke of Wurttemberg, Süss is, in fact, the illegitimate son of a Gentile nobleman. Infamously adapted for the screen in 1940 by the Nazi propagandist machine, *Jew Süss* is a tale of deception and desire and what happens when the human ego runs amok; Süss, found guilty of treason, fraud, lecherous behavior, and deceit, becomes the victim of an angry, anti-Semitic lynch mob and is sentenced to death by hanging. He chooses not to save himself by revealing his noble Gentile origins and dies while reciting the Shema—Hear oh Israel, the Lord Our God, the Lord is One—the most essential prayer in Judaism and the one I fell asleep whispering to myself every night after services at Camp Towanda, as I lay in my little metal cot in rural Pennsylvania, staring at the ceiling joists above me.

Süss had been a master manipulator, a schemer who sold his soul for the sake of power; he broke every commandment, every canon, every tenet, every law handed down to him from Hashem, Blessed Be He, but when it came time for him to meet his maker, the words that dripped from his lips were the most profound and important in the Talmud. Reciting the Shema is part of what makes even the most secular, rule-breaking Jew a Jew, who tethers the fiber of his very being, his self, his heart, to the matriarchs and the patriarchs, to five thousand years of Jewish history and halachic law. It makes him who and what he is. In Süss—Süss the fallen; Süss the condemned; Süss the martyred; Süss the secretly, the privately devout—my father saw himself.

My father believed that I would put down my *From the Mixed-up Files of Mrs. Basil E. Frankweiler* and my *Trumpet of the Swan*, *Tiger Beat* magazines, and my *Wrinkle in Time*; he imagined, somehow, that I would read and fathom this story of deception, of anti-Semitism, of false appearances and desire. He wanted me to believe what he believed: that redemption waited at the end of every Jewish life—even one that had gone completely off the rails.

• • •

I NEVER ACTUALLY SAW MY father read his books—not the forbidden ones on the top shelf in the living room, not the *Reader's Digest* abridged editions on the lower shelves, and not even his beloved Feuchtwanger. He was a newspaper man—the *New York Times* and only the *New York Times*—with, he liked to say, "ink under his finger-nails." He picked up the paper every morning before seven and folded it into thirds; we would sit down at the breakfast counter to-gether, to our soft-boiled eggs and diet white bread and rashers of fatty Oscar Mayer bacon while my mother was putting on her makeup, and he would immediately turn to the obituaries.

"I read them first," he would say, "to make sure I'm still alive." If someone of interest showed up—a famous musician whose work he loved, one of his professors from City College, a shipmate from the Navy, a high school classmate, a colleague from his early days in advertising, a distant publisher cousin who'd been tossed out of the family for some long-forgotten infraction that nobody alive could remember—he clipped them out and stuck them in a file labeled DEAD. Some of the obituaries he deemed important enough to individually seal in plastic ziplock sandwich bags. These were the longer ones—the ones that gave context to their subject's lives. If my father knew them personally, and he often did, he'd read the obituary aloud and then provide his own clarifying com-mentary:

"Morris Pushkin, dead." (No baggie.) "Garment center. Was in my high school air raid group. Bloodied me in the locker room after I tripped him during gym class. A putz who almost got his entire platoon killed in France. Enlisted a putz and came back a putz, with a bullet in his ass and a Purple Heart."

"Lloyd Shearer, dead." (Baggie.) "Second cousin. Newspaper man. Changed his name, became an Episcopalian. No idea why. Hated the family and moved to Beverly Hills. Refused a visit from me. Died a schmuck. Rich and famous; still a schmuck."

"Victor J. Schmittz, dead." (No baggie.) "Roommate, preflight school, Del Monte, California. Went back in, Korea. Surgeon. Mar-ried three times."

My father's dead file, with its ziplocked VIPs who numbered upwards of fifty by the time he moved out, lived in the top drawer of his desk, where, years earlier, I had unearthed Grandpa Philip's gold-embossed Mass card signed by Sister Redempta. My father was completely obsessed with the very end of life. He was gripped by the possibility of redemption itself, like his beloved Süss, and the act of dying with the promise of sanctity and salvation on one's lips.

21

Seven Days

I'M LEANING AGAINST the brown laminate counter at Aunt Sylvia's house on Long Island, both of my hands stuffed up the asses of two kosher chickens.

Clouds of gloom float in and out of the kitchen and swirl around me.

"How could he die," I hear someone moan, "when he was so healthy?"

"What will she do now?" Muffled gasps; tears.

Healthy? I think. He was healthy?

My head is down; I don't respond. Where there is grief, there is delusion.

I feel around for the birds' rib cages and swallow the walnut of sorrow that's been lodged in my throat since Lois called to say that her father was gone. The sleeves of my starched black linen tunic are pushed up to my elbows and I've wrapped myself tightly like a sausage in an old, flowered waist apron left behind two decades earlier when my aunt's longtime Bavarian housekeeper retired, packed up her copies of *Staats-Zeitung*, and went back to Germany. On this hot day in July 1998, my cousins are exhausted and napping; my aunt is in her bedroom, resting her broken heart. Strangers walk around the house and drape every mirror they can find with bed-sheets: an ancient, Orthodox practice requires mirrors be covered as a reminder for the mourners to look to others for sympathy and support. Vanity at such a time is unimaginable. Someone puts a crystal Tiffany pitcher filled with water on the front stoop, for every visitor coming from the cemetery to wash away evil spirits and to reaffirm life. Shiva, the ancient laws say, is a Talmudically sanctioned time to grieve, to look inward, to remember, to receive the compassion, love, and tender care of others without having to ask for it.

When the funeral was over, I took my father's car keys and went to the butcher in town. Not the regular butcher, where Sylvia had been going since she and Uncle Lee moved here, after leaving the split-level they'd lived in when I was a baby. Instead, I go to the kosher butcher, the one whose tzitzit hang out from beneath his stained apron. The meats he sells are strictly glatt—literally, smooth, from animals whose lungs are free of the adhesions that would classify them as treyf, or according to exodus, torn in the field, violently ripped apart, causing death. I buy two huge birds and a first cut brisket big enough to feed an army; I bring only ko-sher foods into this house of mourning. It feels instinctive and pri-mal, as if we, myself included, are suddenly, devout. Our God, the Talmud says, watches over the hearts of the grief stricken; but, I think—Did I hear Grandpa Henry say it one day when he was talk-ing about Hashem? Did it get stuck somewhere in my brain?—per-haps he watches with even a little more attention if the halachic rules and regulations are followed. All of us: we love our French towers of boiled prawns eaten at the Café de la Paix in Paris, our steamed lobsters at the Jolly Fisherman during a birthday celebra-tion, our bits of bacon that cling to the blue cheese in the Cobb salads that we order at our ladies' luncheons, our piles of red-glazed pork ribs at The Tung Shing House. But during shiva, we follow the rules; death is too close not to.

I hunt around the cool damp chicken cavities for the giblets: the liver, the heart, the gorgel, the stomach.

Nothing.

I turn the birds around on Aunt Sylvia's glass cutting board and peel back the long flaps of skin that drape over the place where the necks used to be, and I search for them there; nothing. I plan to do what I always do when I roast a chicken, and something I always find soothing: I put the giblets in a small pan, shower them with a pinch of salt and black pepper, and cook them separately for a quick snack while the bird is roasting. If I'm not hungry, I save them for later. Or I chop them up and add them to pan drippings, with white wine, tarragon, and a little cream. But on this day, with a rabbi sitting in Aunt Sylvia's living room drinking a cup of coffee, cream and chicken—the combination of milk and meat—won't be happening. Even if the rabbi wasn't here, there will be no such treats; the small nuggets of fleshy, meaty flavor—the comforting bits of bird considered by some kosher Jews to be questionable in terms of their cleanliness—are nowhere to be found.

SHIVA; SEVEN DAYS. The weeklong period of mourning for first-degree relatives—parents, children, siblings, spouse; in Hebrew, the avel—of someone who has died. Prior to the funeral service, the rabbi will pin the avel with a black, cloth-covered button attached to a short black ribbon, which is torn in half by the rabbi, representing the rending of garments. First-degree mourners wear the ribbon over the right breast; children are the only ones who wear it over their heart. Food for the shiva is provided by friends and extended family; first-degree mourners are not allowed to serve food to visitors, who are taken care of by others.

We are sitting shiva for Uncle Lee, who, after two years of valiantly fighting congestive heart failure, succumbed to it; it is the day of the funeral and I'm alone in my aunt's vast kitchen, turning out the most mundane of dishes so that the primary mourners—Aunt Sylvia and her daughters—don't have to concern themselves with sustenance while in the throes of grief. The Talmud says to treat mourners gently and with kindness, as though their hearts have been broken, which they have.

The food I produce is plain and unadorned, kind to digestion, more fuel than flavor, and entirely kosher;. This is a time of devotion, and we change the way we eat and cook accordingly; death itself brings us closer to God, and so we become who we're supposed to be and we eat how we're supposed to eat as if our sudden observance of halachic law will compel God to make the transition easier for the dead, and easier for us. If Aunt Sylvia and her daughters get hungry, sustenance will be there, waiting for them: two kosher chickens made the familiar way my grandmothers made them—massaged with a nondescript vegetable oil and paprika and roasted for longer than they by rights should be, because that's the way kosher chickens are cooked in Ashkenazic homes (bloodless; dry). Next to the chickens will be a pot of kosher chicken broth, twice skimmed and crystal clear, ready for the addition of Jewish egg noodles or bits of white meat or kreplach—the meat-stuffed dumplings I once confused with the pork-filled Chinese purses I ate every weekend as a child at the Tung Shing House. There will be a kosher brisket; after I unwrap it from its brown butcher paper, I hunt around Aunt Sylvia's kitchen drawers—it feels wrong to do this, like I'm a thief; I've never felt comfortable taking even a glass of water here without asking first—and come up with a narrow, flexible fillet knife, which I use to make deep slits in the meat, and into which I insert narrow slivers of garlic, the way Grandma Bertha used to do. Rubbed with salt and pepper and garlic powder just the way Sylvia likes it, the meat will braise for five hours—drenched in a bath of tomato sauce and water, and set down on a bed of thinly sliced white onion, the ancient roasting pan tightly sealed with a sheet of heavy-duty aluminum foil—after the chickens come out for a rest. Once they're cool, I will cover the birds in more foil and put them on the shelf in the fridge above the vegetable crisper where, beneath a head of shrink-wrapped broccoli and a bag of green beans, someone has inadvertently left a package of Black Forest ham from Zabar's.

Phyllis, a distant relative who I only ever see at funerals, comes into the kitchen, heads for the nearly-empty Westinghouse coffee urn that was turned on by a neighbor just as the service was starting six hours ago; she eyes me groping around the birds like I'm trying to deliver a foal. She's tall and thick, her chemically straightened, shoulder-length hair dyed an unnatural mahogany, teased up into a tall crown and sprayed into place as if to belie her seventy-five years, her lips smeared with a violent swipe of dense magenta lipstick, wearing a snug Norma Kamali wrap dress left over from the eighties.

"I need more coffee," she demands, thrusting her Styrofoam cup at me.

I nod over my shoulder to the urn across the room, where it's been set up on the oak kitchen table; I'm up to my elbows in chicken juice. She knows exactly what I'm looking for.

"You should know by now," she adds, imperiously, "that kosher birds don't always come with their giblets intact."

"How would I know?" I say, turning around again to look at her.

"I thought you knew everything," she says. "Make more coffee. People are waiting."

She walks out of the kitchen clutching her lipstick-smeared cup.

Fucker, I mumble to myself.

Fuck. Her.

Once, as a child at one of Aunt Sylvia's cocktail parties where I'm playing hide-and-seek in the basement with my younger cousins, I overhear Phyllis call someone a demon seed; there is a tentative, coughing laughter until I walk in to the living room to grab a fistful of Jordan almonds for myself from the silver candy dish on the coffee table. My father's face is red; my mother is in the bathroom, touching up her makeup. After the divorce, after my mother and Ben are married and I spend my holidays and weekends with my father, I long to be a member of this clan, and they cautiously, tentatively let me in; I can taste the sweet essence of family and acceptance, even though somewhere in the recesses of my heart, I fear that I'm a fact of obligation—I am my father's daughter, and when he dies in three years, so will the commitment—who ought to be grateful for being allowed into the pack with everyone else, like a lone wolf who can be shunned at any moment, for the slightest infraction. The demon seed is the imperfect; the treyf; the one who doesn't fit the uniform.

I AM FOREVER ON THE outside, looking in, forever searching and looking for an anchor.

So I cook; I cook to feed them and to nourish them. I cook to feed and nourish myself. I cook as a way to crack open the shell of acknowledgment that I crave. Like my customers at Dean & DeLuca, I cook to re-create the past. I cook as a way to sanctity and peace.

I cook for the living; I cook for the dead.

The cemetery mud cakes the soles of our fancy black dress shoes; Phyllis's conduct breaks the laws of the Talmud—I don't know this for sure, but certainly it must, I think—that say that the grief-stricken, primary mourners and secondary mourners alike should not be treated cruelly and carelessly. But no matter the occasion, happy or sad, birth or death, Phyllis's behavior is always vile, always inappropriate, always bitter, and the subject of discussion among family members who whisper to each over prim layered cakes from William Greenberg's in Manhattan and endless cups of Martinson coffee. But no one will ever be brave enough to call her on it; not her. When Phyllis orders me to make more coffee on the day of Uncle Lee's funeral, I'm gripping one of the chickens from the inside by its rib cage; it's perched on the end of my right hand like a boxing glove. It is greasy and orange with paprika, its legs and wings trussed to its body in bondage, and I imagine flinging it at her like a basketball. I can see it cartwheeling through the air, end over end, and bouncing off the back of her hair-sprayed Jackie Onassis helmet as if off a trampoline, as she sashays coolly out of the room.

THE HOUSE IS FILLED WITH nieces and nephews and grandchildren and neighbors who, like me, also loved Uncle Lee, along with my father and his longtime companion—after fifteen years, calling Shir-

ley his girlfriend feels wrong—and Aunt Sylvia, who sits in her favorite beige velvet armchair, in a daze. We have all been to the chapel,
the one where every deceased member of the family has been me-
morialized, and then, the cemetery, where they are and where the
rest of us will be buried—a family plot where my late cousin Maya
and Grandpa Henry and Grandma Bertha lay shoulder to shoulder
in a sea of Jewish immigrants, mostly from eastern Europe. We keen
and we weep; the rabbi chants The El Malei Rachamim, begging
God for Uncle Lee's rest upon his wings, and my father is inconsol-
able—his well of sorrow is bottomless, his face twisted with grief.
The rabbi, a mottle-haired, slender, gaunt young man not yet forty,
dressed in a navy blue suit that gives off a slight shimmer, davens the
familiar Mourner's Kaddish that I first heard on the mornings after
my grandfather died, when my father and I took the elevator down to
the basement with the dog and he walked me to the school bus stop
at the top of The Champs-Élysées Promenade.

My younger second cousins and I join the rabbi in reciting the
prayer for the dead; I am the only one who has to read it off a card,
phonetically. My father's mouth moves in silent devotion, tears cascade down his face onto the front of his business shirt as Uncle Lee's
kosher casket—all wood, held together with pegs rather than nails,
devoid of any metal that is Talmudically prohibited and symbolic of
war—is lowered into the ground. Each of us is handed the shovel,
and one by one, we participate in chesed shel emet; we shovel
clumps of earth onto the casket, the ultimate act of love and kindness for which the deceased can't ask for himself, and which signi-
fies finality. This is tribal, a five-thousand-year-old ritual and the
fulfilling of what is considered the greatest mitzvah as decreed in the
Talmud. When the service is over, we search the grounds surrounding our family plot for small rocks and pebbles to place on top of
Grandma Bertha's, Grandpa Henry's, and Maya's tombstones, an ancient tradition, an earthly connection to an afterlife that Jews aren't
supposed to believe in. Unsuccessful, we scratch around in the
warm dirt surrounding the graves of total strangers, to unearth something, anything, to leave behind. When she thinks we can't see,

Phyllis palms a rock from the top of a nearby tombstone belonging to
a stranger named Pessie, whose grave is inexplicably located within
the fringes of our plot. Phyllis calls her an interloper; this, Phyllis
believes, gives her the right to take the token that was left perhaps
by a grandchild, or a stranger, for this woman, herself a stranger in a
strange land, buried alone.

Treyf, my father mutters under his breath, wiping his eyes with
his handkerchief. Phyllis gives him a smug, apologetic smile and
shrugs with phony contrition; she thinks he's talking about poor dead
Pessie the gatecrasher.

We leave the rocks; we pat the tombstones. We say goodbye, we
get into our cars, we drive away in a single tidy, ordered line, to begin
the seven-day period of mourning.

THE DELIVERIES ARRIVE ALMOST IMMEDIATELY: there are kosher deli
platters of tongue and turkey and corned beef and pastrami; there is
lox and whitefish and sable and tomato and onion. There are piles of
still-warm miniature knishes that someone sent from the Knish
Nosh, around the corner from The Marseilles: there's potato and
kasha and spinach and liver, which no one eats. There are baskets of
bagels and loaves of rye bread, unseeded because my father and
Aunt Sylvia and at least two cousins have diverticulitis. There are
containers of cream cheese, both vegetable and plain, Gulden's mustard, and jars of half-sour pickles. Every ten minutes, the doorbell
rings, and there's more, first from a local bakery: there are small,
square rainbow cakes, miniature black-and-white cookies, almond
horns, rugelach of three types, a box of mandelbrodt.

Federal express arrives with two separate fruit towers from
Harry & David; someone in the living room shouts to me: Make sure
it's kosher before you put that out.

Ten folding chairs emerge from the basement for the shiva minyan and are organized in a circle near the small settee where Aunt
Sylvia sits, facing the piano and the metronome; ten men plus the
rabbi arrive from the local synagogue, carrying a small, borrowed

Torah scroll sheathed in velvet. The service is held; the rabbi reads, Kaddish is said, the Torah is covered.

My father stands with these men he doesn't know; they are mostly older than he is, a few of them gray-bearded and black-hatted but most of them not. They face east, towards the Long Island expressway and beyond that, eastern Long Island and the wealthy towns of East Hampton and Amagansett and Montauk, where prosperous Jewish families have summered for decades, navigating the ancient quotas and silent restrictions against Jews, finally surrounded by and sucked into the Gentile world around them. They assimilated and assimilated and assimilated again, until they themselves—the thing that made them who they were—were gone and lost to history.

My father and the rabbi and the shiva minyan stand and daven together, bending stiffly at the waist and the knee, mumbling ancient prayers in a deep monotone that sounds like a dull, passing highway rumble. My response is visceral and sudden and uncontrollable; it startles and frightens me, and comes up from my belly, from a place so deep and old that I barely know it. Waves of grief rise and rise again and I hiccup like a baby, gasping for air. This is who I am, I think; this is all I will ever be.

With Uncle Lee gone, my father is now the oldest man in the family, the last patriarch, our closest link to the past. Alongside the old men, he chants the prayers quietly with his bar mitzvah prayer book in his right hand while I stand next to him, weak-kneed and woozy. I slip my arm through his and he doesn't look up; tears roll down his face and onto the pages of his siddur. When it's over, he touches it to the velvet-cloaked Torah, and then to his lips.

22

Susan

MY WIFE, TEN YEARS MY SENIOR, is Catholic, from New England; kind, gray-green eyes the color of autumn moss, the map of Ireland on her freckled face.

When I introduce Susan to my father and Shirley at their condominium, shortly after we meet, my father takes a few giant steps backwards into the living room and falls, as if in slow motion, into his deep wingchair as though he's been dropped into it from the heavens. He groans as he lands and sinks down deeply into the seat, and I recognize the sound of release from my childhood: it's a collapse of exhaustion and finality. Shirley sits on the end of the couch and smiles and cries.

Susan quietly offers my father a drink from his own bar, as though he's a guest in his own home; he grins and says, "Yes. A Gibson." She makes the drink and methodically and slowly walks it over to him, taking care not to spill any of it on the cream broadloom.

"This is the best," he says to her, sipping the clear liquid from the top of the glass, and pulling the pickled onion off the little plastic cocktail sword Susan used as a skewer. He licks his lips to get every last drop and looks at Susan with a combination of surprise and reticent approval, and nods to me with no words, although I know what he means: he didn't know about Julie—nobody did—and I was alone for so long after her, and although I dated men before her, I never brought one person, male or female, out to meet them, or as a guest to Aunt Sylvia and Uncle Lee's holiday parties. It would have been instantly assumed that I was with the person, and that person would be subject to a sort of social inspection, a kind of simian allogrooming over thick slices of coffeecake. Where are your people from? What do you do? Have you considered becoming a physician?

After it's over, Aunt Sylvia and Uncle Lee would have sat my father down over cups of Swee-Touch-Nee tea, and instructed him sternly: Not for her. She needs to find someone else. The way my father himself had to, five times, before he married my mother.

WHILE JULIE WENT HOME TO her family in Minnesota, I would arrive for holiday dinners and family functions dressed in the conservative costumes I knew everyone in my father's family liked. One Thanksgiving at Aunt Sylvia's house, while we're eating pumpkin pie and drinking our tea and our scotch, the doorbell rings and a stout, pale older man with a ginger comb-over—he's forty; I'm twenty-five—steps in; my cousins don't know him, we're all wondering who he is and why he's there. We hear him tell Aunt Sylvia that he can't stay, so he leaves his black, pilling overcoat on. He begins to sweat in the warmth of the house; a Duraflame log burns in the family room. He is dressed in a white business shirt and black tie and bagging black pants and black Velcro loafers that squeak when he walks.

Aunt Sylvia steps back into the dining room. "Elissa," she says, "your ride home is here."

My cousins and I look up from our plates and stare at each other. "What ride?" I say.

"Come," she says to me, "let's get your coat."

I love my cousins and I rarely see them and the party isn't over and I'm still eating and I'm not ready to leave, and I'm not ready to leave with a man nearly twice my age who I've never met before. I glare across the table at my father, who shrugs sheepishly and whispers at me, I have no idea.

There is no scene; no fighting. There are no raised voices.

I put on my tweed overcoat and walk out with this man to his gold sparkling Datsun 280-Z; he opens the immense passenger door and I have to crouch all the way down to reach the molded black leather racing seat. I crush a half-used box of Kleenex under the weight of my leather skirt–clad ass. He slams the door hard; I reach behind me for my seatbelt when the growling begins.

"Don't look at her," he says, pulling out of Aunt Sylvia's driveway, "or it'll get worse."

I turn around. There, perched on a damp wee-wee pad set on top of a royal blue velour bath towel, is a geriatric cocker spaniel, baring her toothless gums at me. Her breath, a phlegmy combination of liver and sour milk, fills the car like a noxious gas. My eyes tear. She shakes her ancient caramel head; her long matted ears flap, spittle flies. The man hands me a plastic container of baby wipes, in case I need them.

"I'm a pediatric dentist," he tells me, looking straight ahead as we drive along the Northern State Parkway.

"I sell cookbooks," I say, holding the box of wipes on my lap. We ride the rest of the way, forty-five minutes into Manhattan, in silence. Except for the snarling.

"Do not ambush me again," I say to Aunt Sylvia on the phone that night, when I call to say I'm home. I am enraged; twenty-five years of familial disapproval bubble up in my throat like bile. I've never spoken this way to her before; I've never put my foot down. I've never said no. There's silence on the other end. She's only trying to help.

"He's the son of my bridge partner," she says. "He's Orthodox, but I don't think it'd be a problem for you."

"I don't care if he's the winner of the fucking Nobel Peace Prize," I say.

Silence.

"You must not be single," she says, under her voice.

She murmurs something about being grateful, and expectation, and dying alone in an apartment with cats, and she hangs up.

FOR YEARS AFTER JULIE, THERE is no one; there are dates with a few women and one man, a friend from work with whom I have an ongoing flirtation. There is sex that means nothing, an explosion of hormones and need. But I spend my days at work, surrounded by twenty varieties of cured pork, and cookbooks, and the promise of sustenance; I spend my nights out with friends, and no matter what, I always come home alone. I have no idea who I am, and I try on costumes to see if they fit: after *Dirty Dancing*, the baggy, shoulder-padded sweater and tight, acid-washed silver gray jeans, the long curly hair, the makeup that delights my mother. The suede-fringed Western jacket and pointed cowboy boots and tooled belt the size of a dinner platter, which reminds me of Forest Hills. The black cotton turtleneck and black cotton leggings and black leather boots from Canal Jeans; my neighbor passes me in the hallway and asks if someone's died. There's the white cotton butcher's apron that I stockpile at Dean & DeLuca, which I had to wear even though I was rarely handling food: at home, I slip the loop over my head and wrap the ribbons twice around my middle and tie it under my navel, and fold a dishtowel into the waistband. I do this the minute I take my coat off, even if no one is coming over for dinner, even if it is just me, which, for years, it is, until I begin to have dinner parties at least once a week, filling my dining room table with hungry colleagues, feeding them, and feeding myself, like the Italian ladies taught me to do near 602.

When I meet Susan, after nine years, I am living in a small studio apartment on the east side of Manhattan. I left Brooklyn on a warm April day; the movers arrived and loaded up my boxes of books and cookware and two huge suitcases and the one piece of furniture that I had left from the apartment I shared with Julie—a massive bookcase that covered an entire wall; it had been dismantled and piled up haphazardly like firewood in my grandparents' living room. My apartment is within walking distance of my new job as a cookbook editor, around the corner from Bloomingdale's, steps away from Central Park, a few blocks from a French butcher named Arnaud, a Puerto Rican kosher butcher, and an Italian fish market serving all of the better restaurants in the city. The day I moved in, the unmistakable odor of ancient chicken fat still hung from my coat sleeves like Christmas tinsel. My first night in my apartment, with no chance of Lipshitz slipping a notice of eviction under my door at three in the morning, or the private detective he hired to follow me waiting outside the building every day, or the ghosts of my grandparents and my cousin floating around me wherever I turned, I slept eighteen hours straight, in my clothes, in my tan suede cowboy boots, with the lights on. At eight o'clock, I passed out cold; the bed was unmade, my box of towels and sheets was buried amidst my stacks of cookbooks on a long wall near the small kitchen. I slept so soundly, so peacefully, that when my mother called the next morning to announce that she was coming over with Ben to take me food shopping with the car, I awoke not knowing where I was: I was no longer in Brooklyn, living in my grandparents' apartment. I was no longer in the Chelsea walkup I shared with Julie. I was in my own home.

The apartment was small and dim, but it was all mine: no Julie, no Lipshitz. My kitchen was a perfect seven-foot square; it was windowless, and the exact size and shape of Gaga's kitchen in The Brussels, with the stove and the refrigerator in the same place. I moved a small wooden table into it, opposite the refrigerator, and placed the French copper cookware from Villedieu, purchased from the store, on top of the wall-hung cabinets above the small sink. The stove was twenty inches across, the dishwasher, eighteen. For the next decade, I cooked my way through the piles of cookbooks that sat on every shelf and sat stacked in every corner: I threw dinner parties for co-workers, for friends, for my bosses, for people I barely knew. I cooked for them; I cooked for myself; I cooked for Gaga.

The day I moved in, my mother waited for the phone company to turn on the service and the cable to be hooked up while I drove out behind the moving truck. She left behind a loaf of white bread, a container of Diamond Crystal salt, and a box of Domino sugar with a note that said, Not to be eaten; for good luck ONLY. The next morning, I broke the rules: I tore into the bread for breakfast and ate it like the sacrament it was, in total silence, sitting on my unmade bed, alone.

MY FATHER CLAIMS, until the day he dies two years later, that Susan made him the finest Gibson he'd ever had. He drank it down quickly and held his glass out to her for another.

Susan makes it and walks it over to him, taking care not to spill any of it.

He drinks it and tries to stand; he topples back into his wingchair.

Susan extends her hand to him and he takes it; she pulls him up.

My father isn't a drinker in his later years; he hasn't been one for a decade—not since the two coronary bypasses and the ileostomy and the prediabetes. Shirley, who is a vegetarian, watches him like a hawk; she allows him a little bit of wine, mostly white, but nothing more. He doesn't ask for alcohol, but tonight, he wants it.

We go out to dinner, to a nearby Italian restaurant, not far from their Long Island condominium; Shirley takes the car keys from the bowl near the front door. My father demands them back. She says no and he says okay, and he doesn't fight her. We eat simply that night: sautéed vegetables and pasta; swordfish; saltimbocca; cannoli. We share an old-fashioned fiasco of white wine. The waiter carries over a tray of Sambuca Romana, and pours out four espressos from an old, battered stovetop moka.

"You're in love," my father says, when Susan gets up to use the restroom. He's tipsy, and slurring his words. Shirley puts her hand on his arm.

"How do you know that?" I ask, pushing the remains of the cannoli around on my plate. I feel my face flush; I can't look at him.

He has never seen me in love before; he doesn't know what I look like in love, and neither do I.

"I can tell," he says, wagging his finger at me. "I remember Emma."

But still, I wait for a rebuke: that she's older. That she's not Jewish. That she's a she.

It never comes.

"What will you tell everybody?" I ask.

I worry; I fret. I have been living on my own for years, and still, I crave Uncle Lee and Aunt Sylvia's approval, which will never come; I want to make them happy with me, which they'll never be; I want to fit the uniform, to be on the inside—safe and secure and right next to Sylvia and my cousins, looking out—rather than on the outside looking in. "It's just as easy to marry a Jewish man as a Gentile man," Sylvia used to say whenever she got the chance. And now I was bringing home a Catholic woman to a family who had never had so much as a Unitarian at their holiday table.

"Vhat's to tell?" my father answers with a Yiddish accent. "It's good."

I hear Grandpa Henry in his voice. My father suddenly looks older; his cornflower blue eyes are bloodshot and tired. He puts his hand over Shirley's and pats it.

"Luff," he says, "is very good."

23

The Plot

THEY ARE BURIED with the Jarczowers, a society of nineteenth-century Orthodox immigrants from Grandpa Henry's hometown of Novyy Yaarchev, who fled pogroms and poverty and, in the case of my grandfather, the violence of the small home he shared with his mother and siblings and new stepfather, to arrive in New York fifty years before the Holocaust. Here, inside the Jarczower Gates—towers of stone bearing the names of the long-dead founders of the society, carved in Hebrew—in a teeming cemetery nestled alongside a crumbling and decrepit racetrack in Queens, are Grandma Bertha and Grandpa Henry, cousin Maya, and now Uncle Lee, who lies beside the plot that will be eventually taken by Aunt Sylvia.

There's the family silver—the set of Gorham Etruscan that every couple received when they married in; there's also the traditional wedding gift of two Jarczower plots among the ancestors, assuring the absolute and final inseparability of the tribe, even as one's bones turned to dust. Grandpa Henry presented my father with a deed for his two plots on the day of his wedding to my mother in 1962; my father quietly sold them both when they divorced. He would no longer be in need of them, he decided, and because his business had failed a year earlier, the money was more important in his pocket. By selling it, he relinquished his eternal connection to the tribe, just as I had when I sold the silver set.

"SHE WAS NEVER ONE OF US anyway," I heard someone say over a platter of cocktail franks at a cousin's engagement party at Aunt Sylvia's house back when I was a teenager. My mother, much of the family believed, had spurned them and took my father away for the sixteen years they were married, making extended family gatherings—birthday parties, Thanksgivings, Passovers—fraught with ugly tension. My mother, Sylvia felt, was contrary, stubborn, argumentative, and resistant to the gorgeous safety and security that my father's family promised. By the time my father moved out and back to 602, Ben was already a part of her life, which became an eddy of boisterous New York City parties and rowdy evenings at Studio 54 and Maxwell's Plum, and cab rides home to The Marseilles in the wee hours of the morning, just as Gaga, who never stopped babysitting my teenage self, nodded off in one of our Louis XVI foyer armchairs while I dozed in my bedroom, my headphones on, Suzi Quatro blaring in my ears.

After the divorce, my father retreated fully into the arms of his family, and with my mother getting involved with Ben, I was hauled into the vortex of Sylvia's family parties and celebrations, ballet recitals and golf outings, vacations and concerts. I craved the order, the safety, the stability of the life that Aunt Sylvia had fashioned for her family. We stepped into her home, where life was formal—almost courtly—and seductively safe: the tribe closed ranks and surrounded me and my father with order and convention; the unexpected and the unplanned were cosmic missteps, aberrations. If the universe presented something that could not be controlled or manipulated, it was simply deleted, like a viral email. With my father and I spending so much time with Aunt Sylvia and Uncle Lee, my life before my parents' divorce grew more and more hazy, as though it was fading from sight in a rearview mirror. My father was one of them and suddenly, inadvertently, so was I, pulled along like a glider plane by circumstance and obligation and what felt to me like love.

DURING THAT TIME, WE WERE a group; a pack. We ran like a herd. We vacationed together, sometimes twenty of us at a time, overrunning resorts all over eastern Florida and the Caribbean. We cooked together and celebrated holidays at Lois's immense French provincial table at her house a mile away from her mother's. At the end of every Passover seder, after the affikomen—the hidden matzo, wrapped in a starched white linen napkin—was found by the youngest child at the table and my father proclaimed, "May the tribe increase," Aunt Sylvia would say, "Children, I want you to remember that we are descended from King David and Maimonides and you"—she pointed around the table to her adult children and their children and my father, and me—"are all mine."

NO ONE IN MY FAMILY is a runner, and neither am I, but on a sweltering August morning the year after 9/11, I went for a run around Lois's neighborhood. I ran hard and fast, wearing worn leather tennis shoes that didn't fit because that's what I'd found buried in the guest room closet at Lois's house. I wanted breathing to hurt. I wanted my heart to explode. I wanted to die before my father. I was tethered to him, and I knew that when I lost him, I would become an unnecessary appendage to the family, a vestige of somebody no longer alive, floating through time and space. Rootless; tribeless.

As I turned the corner onto Palmetto Grove, I saw something in the distance lying in a heap in the middle of the road, swarmed by flies. At first, I thought it was a tattered white rag, or a single filthy sock separated from its owner. As I got closer, I could make out its feathers: a white city pigeon—the kind my father and I used to see perched on the head of the homeless bird man in Central Park, back when my parents' divorce was still fresh—had been hit by a car. It had died violently and suddenly, right there in the middle of a quiet street on a steaming morning on Long Island.

I stopped and knelt by the bird's side; I brushed away the flies, and a guttural bark belched from my lips like a car backfiring. Bunching up a corner of my T-shirt, I picked the pigeon up by its feet and carried it to the park on the next block; its wings unfolded like an accordion, and when I set it down at the base of a Japanese maple, I could see traces of bright crimson streaking its scapular feathers. I covered the bird with a handful of fallen leaves and touched its crown, as if anointing it. It was still warm, its eyes clenched shut.

I ran the half mile back to Lois's house where Susan and I were staying, tears cascading into my mouth, day-old black mascara running off my chin in beads. In two hours, I would remove my father from life support; in two hours, he would be dead. We would gather to mourn over platters of tongue and corned beef ordered in from the kosher deli and eaten with the family silver, as we had done so many times before.

MY FATHER WAS OBSESSED WITH the planes he flew during the war. There was the Grumman F6F Hellcat, the World War I–era biplanes that were so easy to fly that, according to him, everyone in my father's squadron learned on them. The parallel wings let the lightweight plane ride the air like a helium balloon, and kept it there, aloft. They were hard to crash, he said: rolls were safe to do and simple to correct; the planes righted themselves the way a bar of soap, held down in sudsy bathwater by a baby's hands, always pops back up, to the baby's delight.

Years later, when I was a young child and airports were perfect places to entertain small children, he would regularly take me and my mother out for dinner to La Guardia; the odor of jet fuel comingled with the rich food served at the ersatz-fancy window-side restaurants that allowed diners to eat while watching planes take off and land. Dishes—like chicken Kiev, which spurted fountains of butter into the air when you sliced into it, and sticky, stringy duck à l'orange, steak

Diane, and pineapple-glazed ham steaks like what Velma made for Christmas—were cloying and heavy, and teetered on china plates as the roar of the planes taking off rattled the floor beneath our feet.

By the time I was seven, my collection of fake pilot's wings had grown exponentially, and every dinnertime visit to the airport resulted in my adding to my stash; every stewardess walking by had seemingly bottomless pockets full of them to hand out to children, and when they invariably came over to our table, bent down on one knee, and pinned me, I swooned. And then I saluted.

My father loved the food and the show, but mostly, the planes. My mother loathed it.

I grew to be a good, calm flyer over the years because my father had taken pains to explain to me the rules of aerodynamics; it didn't seem possible that anything could bring down a plane, and long after my parents divorced, when we flew together on family trips with Aunt Sylvia and Uncle Lee and hit a nervous-making patch of turbulence, I instinctively checked my father's face for any sign of worry or concern. If he was safe, I was safe. We were all safe.

On the morning of 9/11, my father watched as his beloved planes took down the World Trade Center, as they became weapons of war rather than a fond memory. "I won't live through the year," he told me. He didn't.

MY FATHER AND SHIRLEY WERE driving their maid to her next gig when they were T-boned by four uninsured teenagers doing seventy in a rusted-out Honda Accord. My father's gold, boat-sized sedan spun out and slammed into a streetlight half a block away. Their maid survived, so did Shirley. My father never regained consciousness: not when I sat at his bedside, holding his hand and pleading for him to open his eyes; not when Aunt Sylvia leaned down to his ear to sing his favorite Yiddish song from their childhood, which no one had ever heard her sing before; not when the nurses came in to move his IV because his veins were collapsing; and not when I begged them to be gentle because, all his life, he'd hated needles as a child does, passing out at the sight of them.

"When he gets out of here," Aunt Sylvia promised as we ate hospital cafeteria tuna salad sandwiches on damp, pasty white bread, "I will bring him home to my house, and he will be fine." She nodded and her jewelry clanged together, and she beamed as though everything would be fine; it had to be.

"But he has a home," I said. He and Shirley had been living together for almost twenty years.

"Not mine," Aunt Sylvia said with such clear conviction that, for a moment, I almost believed that she could save him.

The day after the accident, standing in the hallway outside his room in the ICU, a cherubic, baby-faced doctor handed me a clipboard and asked me to sign my father's do not resuscitate order.

Surrounded by Sylvia and Lois, I asked what the chances were of his ever recovering; I choked as the words came out, one by one. "He is already gone," the doctor said. My family gasped; I placed my hand on the wall.

Sylvia, dressed in paisley silk, her lips coated with frosted pink lipstick, hung her head and rested her chin on her chest. The long pendant necklace she wore for luck—four articulated enameled Chinese fish dangling like a fresh catch at the end of a gold rope chain—swung back and forth as she shook her head no, no, no. Her eyes were closed; tears cascaded into her lap. Lois turned and walked away.

I panted and felt disembodied, as if my arms were too long and weighed too much; the floor tilted beneath me and the world began to blacken—I was seeing everything through a darkening scrim. I was fainting; I was dying slowly. I would be without him for the rest of my life, and without him, I would also be without them. Sylvia and I stared at each other, gaping, frozen, tired, and ancient, the weight of our family's primal grief hanging heavy on our shoulders. I would lose my father; she would lose her baby brother. His death, neither of old age nor sickness, could not be contained or controlled. The act of removing him from life support couldn't be tidied up; it couldn't be molded into something other than what it was. No one other than me—my father's next of kin—could do it. Aunt Sylvia, always her little brother's protector and savior, couldn't change his death or revoke it or massage it into beauty; she couldn't safeguard him anymore. In the coming year, she grew distant; a gate tumbled down between us like a rolling postern.

My father would die at my hand; I would break two commandments.

I was treyf.

THE HOSPITAL TOOK CARE OF his needs while he lay in a coma, shaving him and bathing him, but they forgot his hands, which had begun to peel and crack with dryness; holding them, I felt our past—the hands that held the hot frying pan handle in Forest Hills, washing the incendiary bacon grease out from our breakfast skillet under a stream of cool Queens tap water; the hands that grabbed the boiled brain out from beneath my wide-eyed stare at 602; the hands that curled into a fist when I misbehaved, sending me sprawling to the sticky bathroom floor at the Tung Shing House; the hands that grabbed Tor's collar at Velma and Buck's Christmas celebration; the hands that touched his prayer book to the Torah and brought it to his lips.

We buried him in the Jarczower plot, not far from his mother and father and Uncle Lee; he wore his childhood bar mitzvah tallis, which, Shirley said, he had begun wearing every morning when he faced east out their condominium den windows, across the suburban tennis courts he had lusted for when I was a child. Every morning towards the end of his life, Shirley said, he davened the Shacharit, just as Grandpa Henry had done every day of his life. No one but she knew, or saw him do it.

A year after he died, we returned to the cemetery for the unveiling of my father's tombstone, which had been engraved with the Star of David on one side and his naval wings on the other. I held Susan's hand and wept while we listened to the rabbi chant the ancient El Malei Rachamim. We gathered pebbles and rocks and set them on the top of the stone; we patted it. We said goodbye. And I crossed the line from tribal member to stranger; my earthly connection to my father was gone and, with it, my place in the family order.

When the unveiling was over, I stopped into the cemetery office to ask about the remaining Jarczower plots.

The office manager pecked at his computer keyboard; he pushed up his reading glasses and shook his head.

"No. Nothing left."

The family plot was closed.

24

Treyf

You only are free when you realize
you belong no place—you belong every place—
no place at all.

—Maya Angelou

THE CONNECTICUT HOME I share with Susan is neither suburban nor rural; drive three miles in one direction, and crumbling New England barns—some red, some silvered maple fashioned from planks milled in the eighteenth century—dot the rolling landscape, partitioned like a patchwork by old stone walls. Drive three miles in the other direction and prefabricated strip malls line the main road; Starbucks, Best Buy, Dunkin' Donuts, Domino's Pizza, and nail salons repeat in an endless loop. Where we live, the modern abuts the ancient, each a constant reminder of the other.

"Don't put your name on the mailbox," my father said when I first left New York in 2001, to be with Susan a year after we met. Back then, she lived in a small Connecticut village of thirty-five hundred—it had gotten its first stoplight in 1996; they had a known black bear problem, a moose who strolled up her street from the thicket of woods below, and a neighbor who kept in his front yard sixteen vehicles including a small yacht on which he would sit in a folding chair every Sunday morning to read the local paper. There was a Catholic church on one corner, two Congregational churches a mile in both directions from the house, and a stone Anglican church seven miles down the road.

I was the only Jew for miles.

"They don't care that I'm here, Dad," I said when he voiced concern, and nobody did. I was sure of that.

"Do you?" he asked. I didn't.

I had flunked out of Hebrew school on the first day, never set foot in a synagogue except for weddings, funerals, and bar mitzvahs, and was fed the promise of assimilation from everyone around me: from Gaga, who was so enraptured with Christmas that she hauled me to St. Patrick's Cathedral every holiday to stand in line for a glimpse of the Baby Jesus rendered in papier-mâché. From Aunt Sylvia, who turned away from a genetic memory of pogroms and annihilation and towards an upper-class American future of finery and wealth and safety. From my father, whose childhood connection to religion was sheathed in violence and chronic disappointment, who vehemently fed me treyf from the time I could eat solid food, because, he believed, I would ultimately become what I ate. All of them, without even knowing it, struggled to create a facade of perfection that would shield them—us—from the specter of our catastrophic history, and help us gain acceptance to a club to which we'd only been tentatively invited. All of us broke our culture's commandments and frayed the tether to convention, as a path towards transcendence.

In rural New England, a million miles away from New York, no one seemed to care who or what I was. Deep in the country, when the power goes out and you need to borrow a generator, or you have a snow plow and the person next door to you doesn't in the midst of a blizzard, very few people think about anything but just being a good neighbor. At least mine didn't.

• • •

I MOVED TO NEW ENGLAND from East Fifty-Seventh Street in New York, where I lived just two blocks away from Central Synagogue, one of the oldest shuls in continuous operation in the city; built in a Moorish style that smacked, I thought, of an always-present connection to Spain, the Inquisition, and the expulsion, the magnificent old temple loomed over Lexington Avenue, and every morning during the workweek, I was inexplicably drawn to the route that would take me past it, like metal to magnet, although I could have gone another way. One late Friday afternoon, shortly after Ben died suddenly of a massive stroke, I walked home from work by way of Central; Shabbos services were just about to start. I climbed the stairs, stepped inside, and was greeted by a warm-eyed slender man who introduced himself as Peter Rubinstein, the rabbi.

"Please stay if you'd like," he said, putting on his tallis.

I sat down near the back and looked up at the stained glass and at the old tiles under my feet. It was an ordinary Friday night; no particularly holiday. The shul was practically empty. The Shabbos candles were lit; the prayer was said.

Baruch atah, Adonai, Eloheinu, melech haolam, asher
kid'shanu b'mitzvotav, v'tzivanu l' hadlik ner shel Shabbat.

I closed my eyes and listened to the Aleinu, which I remembered from my Friday nights at camp in the 1970s, safe from the wildness at home in The Marseilles; I stood to recite the Mourner's Kaddish for Ben, transliterated in the siddur. Tears spontaneously poured down my cheeks and into the collar of my shirt; I tried to hide my face. An older man standing behind me put his hand on my shoulder and leaned down.

"It's okay," he whispered. "We all weep—we're Jews."

A year later, on Shabbos, a fire broke out in the sanctuary; I was passing the synagogue on my way home from work when billows of smoke blew through the roof. The rabbi who had been so kind to me flew across the street from the Hebrew school, wildeyed, dodging on-coming taxis. A crowd gathered and watched as he put a handker-

chief over his face, flung open the doors of the shul, ran in, and moments later, ran out, coughing, the Holocaust memorial Torah
cradled in his arms. We stood on the north side of the street, our
faces cocked to the sky, as the flames destroyed the building; I
stepped back towards the school as the firemen began to arrive.
Watching the synagogue burn felt ancient and tribal, and from another time and place; we could have been anywhere: Novyy Yarchev.
Vilna. Vienna. Manhattan.

Someone shouted my name behind me; I turned around and my
mother was there, having arbitrarily decided, a few months after her
second husband died, to come to Central Synagogue on that particular night, to say Kaddish for Ben. I stood in front of her and together
we watched the flames in silence, her arm resting protectively across
my chest, the tightest she's ever held me against her.

THE CHRISTMAS AFTER I BROUGHT the pig home, I submerged the
shoulder in two gallons of spiced dork—duck and pork—fat for three
days, confiting it in the traditional French style; while the snow fell,
I roasted it outside, on the grill, until the skin popped and crisped
and darkened to a pink-flecked umber, and the fat that had encased
the meat sent billows of gamey smoke into the air. Dogs howled;
neighbors and friends came over and pulled mindlessly at the meat
with their forks, wrapping it up in warm flatbread, the crunch and
the tender together, hot pig grease dripping off their chins. A month
later, in the dead of winter, I marinate a butt in sour orange juice and
achiote paste, wrap it in moistened banana leaves, and slow-roast it
for hours in Lois's old Römertopf; we eat spicy cochinita pibil for
days. I spend weeks perfecting a recipe for brasato di maiale al latte;
I stand at our sink, Grandma Bertha's old, chicken fat–infused walnut cupboard hovering over me like a drone, while I massage this
gorgeous hunk of heritage Tamworth pork—this animal who was
grown for us by a stranger, with all the blitheness of a second grader
growing an avocado plant—with raw milk. It teeters and wobbles in
the sink, its straight grain of dark pink meat streaked with bright fat

that my wife wants me to slice away so that she can render the lard. Somewhere, in a place I can't name, I reach my tipping point; hot Levitical fury pants down the back of my neck; I close my eyes and hear strains of my grandfather davening all those years ago, at the tiny, stuffy shul in Coney Island, expunging the demons that he carried over from Novyy Yaarchev, too mesmerized by prayer, too beguiled by ghosts, too in love with God to recognize his own son.

I weep silently over the sink; I am the real, modern American, the one who transcended my family's genetic code of violence and rage and disappointment, who broke every Talmudic law presented to us as though it was our job. I am no longer saddled with an impractical, demanding piety five thousand years old; I am the one who lives and eats—unfettered by my family history of death, longing, guilt, shame, and the relentless desire to belong—like a Gentile living in a Gentile world. Am I not who they struggled to be? Am I not who they wanted me to become?

Belonging everywhere, I now belong nowhere.

On this night, I stand in my Connecticut kitchen, in our house, with my Catholic wife in the next room, listening to my father's favorite Chopin Étude, our dogs asleep at her feet. I am safe—finally safe—even as I yearn for him, and for Gaga, and for Grandpa Henry, and for all who came before me.

To know who I am; to remember where I came from.

ACKNOWLEDGMENTS

My grateful thanks to Adriana Stimola at Stimola Literary Studio, Open Road Media, Sharon Bowers at Miller Griffin Bowers, and Berkley Books. Thanks to Fine Arts Work Center in Provincetown, Barnswallow Books, Tin House, Vermont Studio Center, and Corsicana Writers and Artist Residency for the gift of time and space to write. Thanks to my memoir students, and to my teachers, mentors, and friends Charles D'Ambrosio, Dani Shapiro, Bonnie Friedman, Linda Wells, Sydny Miner, RF Jurjevics, Jacqueline Church and Caleb Ho, Louise and Mark Carpentier, Stevie and Porter Boggess. Grateful thanks to the Jewish Book Council, and for English to Yiddish translation assistance, Eve Sicular and Yankl Salant. Abundant thanks to my friends from Forest Hills, Manhattan, the Catskills, Pennsylvania, Connecticut, and beyond, and for my extended family by both blood and affection, especially the Schwartzes, the Londons, the Fertigs, the Fiebers, the Puchkoffs, the Turners, the Deans, the Sindlands, the Hopkins, the Cassellas. Deepest thanks to my parents, Rita Hammer, the late Buddy Hammer, Shirley Puchkoff, and the late Cy Altman, and to my beloved Susan Turner.

E.M.A.
2023

ABOUT THE AUTHOR

ELISSA ALTMAN is the James Beard Award–winning author of the memoirs *Motherland*, *Treyf*, and *Poor Man's Feast*. A finalist for the Lambda Literary Award, Connecticut Book Award, and Maine Literary Award for memoir, Altman's work has appeared in *Orion*, *On Being*, *O: The Oprah Magazine*, *LitHub*, the *Wall Street Journal*, *Dame*, *Lion's Roar*, *The Guardian*, and the *Washington Post*, where her column, *Feeding My Mother*, ran for a year. Altman writes and speaks widely on the intersection of sustenance, nature, and the creative spirit, and has appeared live on the TEDx stage and at the Public Theater in New York. She teaches the craft of memoir widely, including at the Fine Arts Work Center in Provincetown, Maine Writers & Publishers Alliance, and at the university level. She lives in Connecticut with her family.

ELISSA ALTMAN

FROM OPEN ROAD MEDIA

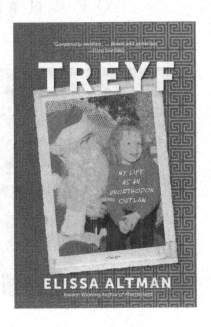

OPEN ROAD

INTEGRATED MEDIA